Windows® 95 On the Job™ Essentials

Laura Acklen

Que E&T

Windows® 95 On the Job Essentials

Library of Congress Catalog No.:

ISBN: 1-57576-249-8

98 97 96 95 4 3 2 1

Interpretation of the printing code: the rightmost double-digit number is the year of the book's printing; the rightmost single-digit number, the number of the book's printing. For example, a printing code of 95-1 shows that the first printing of the book occurred in 1995.

Screens reproduced in this book were created using Collage Plus from Inner Media, Inc., Hollis, NH.

Publisher: David P. Ewing

Publishing Director: Charles O. Stewart III

Acquisitions Editor: Rob Tidrow

Managing Editor: Jenny Watson

Cover Designer: Ann Jones

Book Designer: Paula Carroll

Production Editor: Theresa Mathias

Production Team: Georgiana Briggs, Mona Brown, Michael Brumitt, Jeanne Clark, Amy Cornwell, Terrie Deemer, Louisa Kluzcnik, Kevin Laseau, Brian-Kent Proffitt, Tina Trettin, Mark Walchle

Developed by Gail Perry

Technical review by Mike Stanley

Composed in *Stone Serif* and *MCPdigital* by Que Corporation

About the Author

Laura Acklen is an independent author and instructor located in Austin, Texas. She has been training and supporting computer users in DOS and Windows products since 1986. She is the author of Que's *WordPerfect 6.0 SureSteps* and co-author of *Oops! WordPerfect...What To Do When Things Go Wrong*. She is also a contributing author of *Special Edition Using WordPerfect Version 6 for Windows*, and the revision author for *Windows QuickStart, 3.11 Edition*. Her most recent projects include Que's *First Look at Windows 95* and Que Education's *Windows 3.1 Essentials, WordPerfect 6.1 for Windows Essentials,* and *Windows 95 Essentials.*

Acknowledgments

Que Education and Training would like to thank the following people: long-time computer-book author and trainer Laura Acklen, for cheerfully creating first-rate instructional material on a tight schedule once again; training specialist Jeff Nelson-Folkersen, for crafting a superb *Instructor's Manual* to accompany this workbook while also ensuring the accuracy and pedagogical soundness of the latter; Rob Tidrow, for the acquisitions efforts on this project in the midst of his own own many writing and development projects; training professional Gail Perry, for ensuring that this book would meet the needs of adults learning Windows 95; Jenny Watson, for managing the production schedule and making sure the project ran smoothly; and Que alumna Theresa Mathias, for a wonderfully attentive job of long-distance editing.

Preface

Que Education and Training is the educational publishing imprint of Macmillan Computer Publishing, the world's leading computer book publisher. Macmillan Computer Publishing books have taught more than 20 million people how to be productive with their computers.

This expertise in producing high-quality computer tutorial and reference books is evident in every Que Education and Training title we publish. The same tried-and-true authoring and product development process that makes Macmillan Computer Publishing books bestsellers is used to ensure that training materials from Que Education and Training contain the most accurate and most up-to-date information. Experienced and respected software trainers write and review every manuscript to provide class-tested pedagogy. Quality-assurance editors check every keystroke and command in Que Education and Training books to ensure that instructions are clear and precise.

Above all, Macmillan Computer Publishing and, in turn, Que Education and Training have years of experience in meeting the learning demands of adult users in business and at home. We offer tiered courseware that:

- Provides broad-based, flexible training for novices through expert users
- Is anchored in the practical and professional needs of *adult learners*
- Includes ample trainer support in fully annotated *Instructor's Manuals*

The "Essentials" of Hands-On Learning

The two-color, spiral-bound *Essentials* series is the choice for instructors training in application basics. Ideal for short courses—from a few hours to a full day or more—this series is custom-tailored to the needs of *adult learners.* The *Essentials* enable users to become self-sufficient quickly; encourage self-learning after training; maximize learning through clear, complete explanations; and serve as desk references after training. They are designed to facilitate instruction and maximize learning by an emphasis on "applied" training. In addition, the *Essentials* help reduce the amount of follow-up support needed after adult learners leave the training room. Each *Essentials* module is two-color throughout, measures 8 1/2"×11" for maximum screen-shot visibility, has 200 pages, and contains a disk with the data files needed to complete the exercises. Each *Essentials* contains the following key elements:

- ***Project Objectives*** list what learners will do and learn from each project.
- ***"Why Would I Do This?"*** shows learners why this material is essential.
- ***Step-by-Step Tutorials*** simplify the procedures with large screen shots, captions, and annotations.
- ***If You Have Problems...*** anticipates common pitfalls, and advises learners accordingly.
- ***Inside Stuff*** provides tips and shortcuts for more effective applications.
- ***Key Terms*** are highlighted in the text and defined in the margin when they first appear.
- ***Jargon Watch*** offers a layman's view of "technobabble" in easily understandable terms.
- ***Concepts Sidebars*** occasionally showcase intriguing topics.
- ***Applying Your Skills*** contains directed, hands-on exercises to check comprehension and reinforce learning.
- ***Data Disks*** contain files for the text's step-by-step tutorials.

Instructor's Manual

The Instructor's Manual is an ideal companion guide to workbooks in the Essentials series. It includes teaching concepts and procedures, strategies for structuring content and organizing the class, ideas for adapting the material for various audiences, pre-training assessment and post-class evaluation tools, and much more. The backbone of the Instructor's Manual is a heavily annotated student workbook that serves as an indispensable resource for trainers. New trainers will appreciate the tips that help them teach a topic successfully for the first time. Experienced trainers will appreciate fresh approaches to teaching familiar topics.

About This Workbook

Welcome to the *Windows 95 On the Job Essentials* workbook! The *On the Job Essentials* series consists of student workbooks and instructor manuals for use in instructor-led, corporate training classes.

If this is your first experience with instructor-led training, you're in for a real treat. Instructor-led, hands-on training is the fastest and most efficient means of teaching software applications. Your instructor is an expert in this application, so he/she can answer your questions and pass on valuable advice about using the software. What all this means is that with the use of these materials, you'll be up and running in the shortest amount of time possible.

Who Should Use This Book?

The *On the Job Essentials* workbooks are designed to be used in the corporate training environment, which means special attention is given to the needs of adult learners in the workplace. Most of us don't have the time to sit down and learn *all there is to know* about a program. We aren't working towards a degree, and we don't like to study! To address this issue, the projects in the *Essentials* workbooks are designed to teach only the "bare essentials"—just enough for you to get the job done.

To ensure your success with Windows 95, you should have a basic understanding of the computer. This workbook assumes you are familiar with the keyboard, the monitor, the floppy drives, and the mouse. This workbook *does not* assume any prior knowledge of the Windows program.

How To Use This Book

Because an instructor will be present in the classroom, the *Essentials* workbooks contain a minimum of explanation and the maximum of step-by-step directions. As you begin each project, you are told what you want to accomplish and why. Realistic examples are given so you can quickly relate to the task and see the value of completing the project.

Each lesson is a series of separate projects with detailed instructions to guide you through the completion of a task. After each numbered step, a brief explanation of the action is given to help you really understand "why you just did that." At the end of each project, tips and shortcuts are given to satisfy the more curious reader. A summary table is included at the end of each lesson to give you a quick reference you can use later when you need a quick refresher.

To make your learning experience as enjoyable as possible, the projects are task-oriented, and they use real-world, business examples.

Task-Oriented Lessons

The workbook lessons are task-oriented, which means you will actually accomplish a task as you work through the lesson. For example, instead of merely *reading* about moving and copying files, you learn how to work with files by actually moving and copying files onto a floppy disk. Likewise, you learn how to customize the Windows program by turning on the screen saver, setting the clock, and adjusting the speed of your mouse.

Once you get past the first two projects, the remaining projects are independent of the others, so they can be completed in any order. If your time is limited, you can pick and choose your projects, depending on which concepts you need to learn right away.

Real-World Examples

The examples used in the *On The Job Essentials* series are geared for the corporate audience. Concepts are illustrated with realistic situations that you would encounter in a workplace. The more realistic the examples are, the easier it is for the reader to relate to the situation. For example, in the steps to create a new folder, the name of the new folder is **Loan Documents**, rather than **Sample Folder**.

Another example: in the lessons where you learn how to open and arrange windows, popular Windows 95 applets (WordPad and Paint) are used, rather than the Windows games. The benefit here is two-fold: you learn how to open and arrange windows and you are introduced to two important applications that come with the Windows program.

Conventions Used in This Book

The On The Job Essentials books use the following conventions to make it easier for you to understand the material:

- Text that you are to type appears in **boldface**.
- Underlined letters in menu names, menu commands, and dialog box options appear in a different color. Examples are the **P**rograms menu, the **C**ontrol Panel command, and the **W**allpaper list box.
- Important words or phrases are in *italic* the first time they are discussed.
- *Key terms* are briefly defined in the margin as soon as they are introduced.
- On-screen text and messages appear in a `special font`.
- *If you have problems...* boxes contain troubleshooting tips that anticipate common pitfalls. These are designed to help you solve your own problems so you can keep up with the rest of the class.
- Jargon Watch boxes are used to define a group of key terms used in the project.
- Inside Stuff boxes contain tips and shortcuts to help you use the application more effectively.

Table of Contents

Project 1

Getting Started with Windows 95

Objectives

In this project, you learn how to

- Start Windows
- Use the Mouse
- Identify the Elements of a Window
- Use the Menu Bar
- Use Dialog Boxes
- Use the Help System
- Exit the Windows Program

Why Would I Do This?

Compared to most DOS character-based programs, Windows programs are easier and more natural to learn and operate. With Windows programs, you experience decreased learning time, fewer mistakes, and easier transition between Windows programs. In fact, studies show that people who use graphical user interfaces (GUIs), such as Windows, use three times as many programs in their daily work as people who use character-based programs. Windows programs can make you more efficient, more productive, and more valuable at work or in school.

Whether you are new to personal computers or just new to Windows, this project helps you get started. In this project, you learn how to start and exit the Windows program. You learn how to use the mouse, how to identify the different parts of a window, and how to make choices in the menus and dialog boxes. Finally, you learn how to use the Windows Help system so you can get quick answers to your Windows questions. If you have experience with personal computers or with Windows, some of this material might be familiar to you.

Lesson 1: Starting Windows

The first thing you need to know about Windows is how to start the software. In this lesson, you learn how to start Windows; however, before you can start Windows, it must be installed on your computer. If you need to install Windows, refer to your Windows manual or ask your instructor for assistance.

In most cases, Windows starts automatically when you turn on your computer. If your system is set up differently, you must start Windows from the DOS prompt (such as `C:\>`). Try starting the Windows program now.

To Start Windows

1 Turn on your computer and monitor.

Most computers display technical information about the computer and the operating software installed on it. If Windows starts, you can skip step 2. Otherwise, you see the DOS prompt `C:\>`.

2 At the DOS prompt `C:\>`, type win and then press Enter.

When you start the Windows program, a Microsoft Windows 95 banner displays for a few seconds; then the desktop appears (see Figure 1.1).

Figure 1.1
The Windows 95 desktop appears a few seconds after a Windows 95 banner.

If you have problems...

If your computer is connected to a network, you might need to *log on* to Windows. If this is necessary, a message appears (after the Windows 95 banner) requesting a user name and password. After you supply this information, Windows starts. See your instructor if you have any questions. Your screen might look different from Figure 1.1 if your copy of Windows has been set up differently.

In Windows, the computer screen is called the *desktop*. The My Computer and Recycle Bin *icons* always appear. If your computer is connected to a network, you also have a Network Neighborhood icon on the desktop. Other icons might also appear, depending on how your system is set up.

Shortcuts to frequently used objects (such as documents, printers, and network drives) can also be placed on the desktop. A shortcut is represented by an icon with a small arrow in the icon's lower-left corner. Figure 1.1 shows a shortcut to the Word for Windows program.

The *taskbar* appears at the bottom of the desktop, but you can move the taskbar to the top, left, or right of the desktop by dragging it. The *Start button* appears at the left end of the taskbar. Clicking the Start button opens the Start menu, which gives you access to your programs, recently opened documents, settings, the Find utility, and the Windows Help system. You can also use options on the Start menu to run programs and shut down Windows.

Jargon Watch

You had to wade through a lot of computer jargon in Lesson 1, probably your first experience using Windows. Throughout this book, key terms are defined where they are first used. When a number of computer terms are introduced in the same lesson, they are defined in a Jargon Watch box like this one.

A **graphical user interface** (or **GUI**, usually pronounced GOO-ee) is a computer application that uses pictures, graphics, menus, and commands to help users communicate with their computers. This is contrasted with a text mode interface where everything is done with words and letters, rather than pictures.

The terms **application** and **program** are interchangeable. Both refer to computer programs, like WordPerfect or Excel, which are instructions that tell the computer how to operate and what to do when you choose a command.

An **icon** is a picture that represents an application, a file, or a system resource. A **shortcut** gives you quick access to frequently used objects so you don't have to look through menus each time you need to use that object.

Lesson 2: Using the Mouse

Windows is designed to be used with a pointing device, such as a mouse, trackball, or finger-pointing device. In most cases, you will be working with a mouse, so it's important that you learn how to use a mouse correctly. With a little practice, using a mouse is as easy as pointing to something with your finger.

A mouse has many functions in Windows and Windows applications. You can use the mouse to select icons, to make selections from *pull-down menus* and *dialog boxes*, and to select objects you want to move or resize.

Your mouse might have either two or three buttons. The left mouse button is called the *primary mouse button*. Unless you are instructed otherwise, use the left button throughout the projects in this book. Practice using the mouse now.

Jargon Watch

The left button is referred to as the **primary mouse button** because you use it most of the time. Windows uses **pull-down menus**, which cascade downward into the screen whenever you select a command from the menu bar; and **dialog boxes**, which open on-screen when you need to enter more information to complete a command.

To Use the Mouse

1 Move the mouse across your desk or mouse pad

As you move the mouse, the mouse pointer (refer to Figure 1.1) moves across your screen in the same direction.

❷ Move the mouse pointer to the My Computer icon on the desktop.

Make sure the mouse pointer is positioned directly over (on) the icon before you proceed to the next step. You can position the mouse pointer on the picture of the computer or the words `My Computer`.

❸ Click the left mouse button.

If you click the left mouse button once, you select an item—in this case, the My Computer icon. When you single-click an icon, you tell Windows that this is the icon you want to work with. The My Computer icon is now highlighted, which means it is the selected icon. Leave the mouse pointer over the icon for the next step.

❹ Click the right mouse button.

Clicking the right mouse button opens the Context menu for the My Computer icon (see Figure 1.2). Context menus are used all over the Windows program.

Throughout the lessons in this book, the term *right-click* is used to describe pointing to something and clicking the right mouse button.

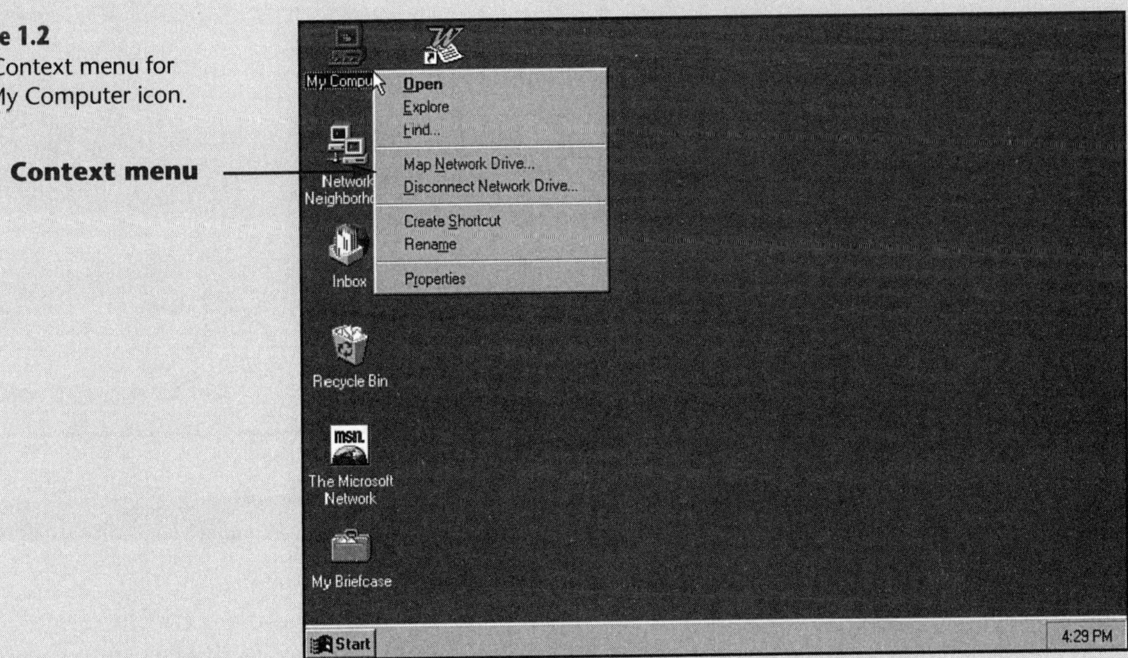

Figure 1.2
The Context menu for the My Computer icon.

❺ Right-click the desktop.

This clears the Context menu for the My Computer icon and opens the Context menu for the desktop. These menus are *context-sensitive*, which means the menu changes, depending on what you are pointing to when you click the right mouse button.

continues

To Use the Mouse (continued)

6 Click the desktop anywhere outside the Context menu.

This time you should use the left mouse button. Clicking the desktop clears the Context menu.

7 Point to the My Computer icon, then double-click the left mouse button.

When you double-click with the left mouse button, the My Computer application starts. The My Computer application opens in a *window* on the desktop, as shown in Figure 1.3. (The next lesson discusses windows in more detail.) Notice that a My Computer button has been added to the taskbar.

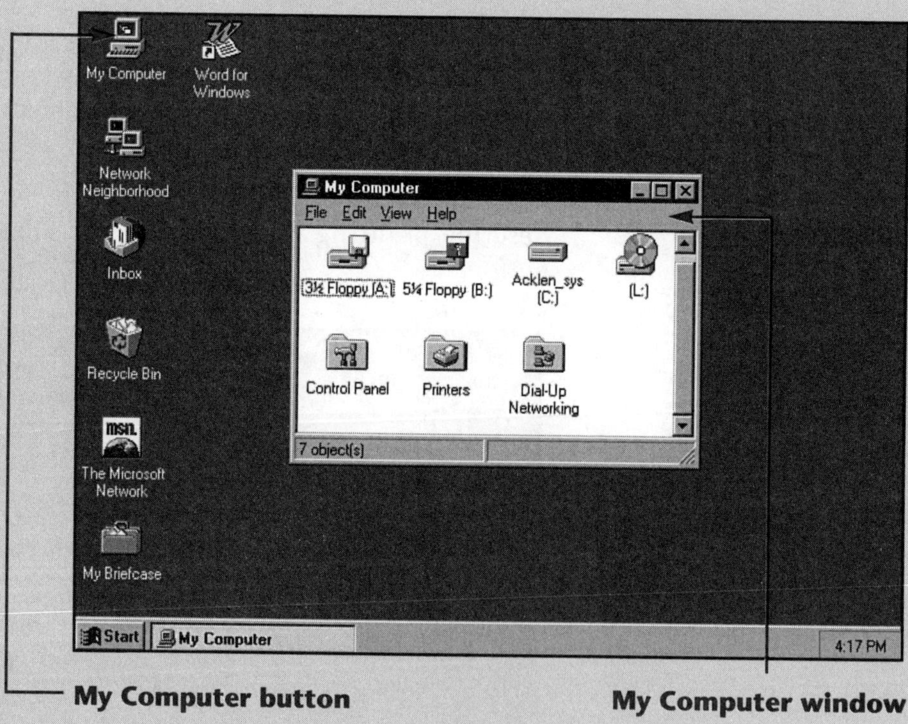

Figure 1.3
Double-clicking the My Computer icon opens the My Computer application in a window on the desktop.

To Drag and Drop Objects

Another mouse technique you will often use is drag and drop. On the desktop, you can use the drag-and-drop technique to move icons and windows to different locations. In My Computer, you can drag and drop files to move and copy them to new locations. In word processing applications, you can drag and drop sections of text to new locations in a document.

To *drag and drop*, you position the mouse pointer over an item (such as an icon, selected text, or a graphic image). Press the left mouse button and hold it down while you move the mouse pointer to a new location. When you release the left mouse button, the object drops to its new location. This technique is different from a simple click, where you move the mouse pointer to an item and then quickly click and release the mouse button.

You will use the drag-and-drop technique often in all your Windows applications, so practice this technique now.

1 In the My Computer window, position the mouse pointer over the top-right icon.

In Figure 1.3, this is the CD-ROM (L:) drive icon, but it doesn't really matter which icon you select here. Then press and hold down the left mouse button.

2 With the left button still held down, drag the icon to the right until part of the icon disappears behind the right border of the My Computer window.

3 Release the left mouse button.

Releasing the left mouse button drops the icon into its new position. You should be able to see only a portion of the icon. Notice the scroll bars in the My Computer window (see Figure 1.4). Scroll bars appear when you have more information—in this case, icons—in a window than is currently displayed on-screen.

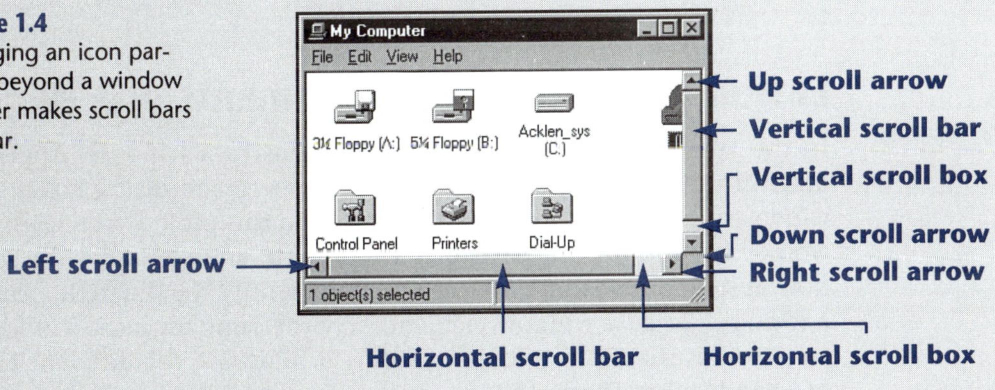

Figure 1.4 Dragging an icon partially beyond a window border makes scroll bars appear.

4 Click the right scroll arrow on the horizontal scroll bar.

When you click the right scroll arrow, it creates the illusion of moving the My Computer window to the right, making visible part of what is beyond the right border of the window. You use the scroll arrows at either end of the horizontal scroll bar to move the window right or left. Similarly, you use the scroll arrows at either end of the vertical scroll bar to move the window up or down.

5 Click the down scroll arrow on the vertical scroll bar.

Clicking the down scroll arrow creates the illusion of moving the My Computer window down. Scroll back to the top of the window now.

continues

To Drag and Drop Objects (continued)

6 Click the up scroll arrow on the vertical scroll bar.

Click the up scroll arrow to move the My Computer window up until you see the icons at the top of the window again.

Now, practice the drag-and-drop technique again as you drag and drop back into position the drive icon you moved earlier.

7 Using the drag-and-drop technique, move the drive icon back to its original position.

You should now be familiar with the most commonly used mouse techniques. In the next lesson, you learn how to identify the different parts of a window.

INSIDE Stuff

If you are left-handed, you can switch the order of the left and right mouse buttons. See Lesson 4 in Project 6, "Customizing Windows," for more information.

When you practice using the scroll bars, notice how the *scroll box* moves up or down on the vertical scroll bar as you move up or down through what you see in the window. If you scroll down to the farthest limit of what you can see in a window, the scroll box appears at the bottom of the scroll bar. You can click and drag scroll boxes to move quickly through a window.

Lesson 3: Identifying the Elements of a Window

In the Windows program, everything opens in a window. Applications open in windows, documents open in windows, and dialog boxes open in windows. As you work through the lessons in this project, you learn how to work with the different parts of a window (to arrange, move, or size). For now, it's important that you learn how to identify the different elements of a window. Because window elements stay the same for most windows, this section uses the My Computer window to illustrate the different elements of a window (see Figure 1.5).

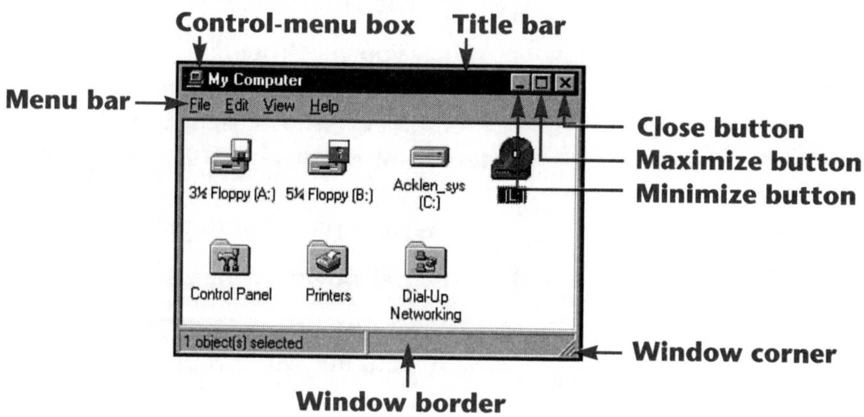

Figure 1.5
The My Computer window has window elements found in all Windows applications.

Table 1.1 describes each of these window elements.

Table 1.1 Window Elements

Element	Function
Title bar	Displays the name of the window or the document in the window.
Menu bar	Displays a list of the menus from which you can choose.
Control-menu box	Accesses a menu that enables you to choose commands to control the window, including changing the window size, closing a window, and switching to a different window.
Maximize button	Expands the active window to fill the entire screen.
Minimize button	Shrinks the window to an icon at the bottom of the screen.
Close button	Closes the window.
Window border	Identifies the edge of the window. You can drag the window border to change the size of most windows.
Window corner	Used for resizing the window. Dragging the corner resizes two sides at the same time on most windows.
Mouse pointer	Moves on your screen when you move the mouse on your desk. Move the mouse pointer to the item you want to choose (or select) on your desktop.

Try to identify the parts of a window now.

To Identify the Elements of a Window

Locate each of the following elements on your screen:

a. The window border

b. The menu bar

c. The Maximize button

d. A window corner

e. The Minimize button

f. The title bar

g. The Control-menu box

Lesson 4: Using the Menu Bar

Windows commands are organized into *pull-down menus*. You pull down (or open) a menu by choosing the menu name on the menu bar. The menu name describes the type of commands on that menu. After you open a menu, you can choose a menu command from the list. You can use both the mouse and the keyboard to open menus and choose menu commands.

You use pull-down menus to perform various functions in Windows applications, including saving files, editing and formatting documents, and accessing the Help system. Because menu bars in Windows applications have similar commands and you use the same methods to choose menu options, other Windows applications are easier to learn. Practice opening and choosing menu commands now.

To Use the Menu Bar

1 Click the drive C: icon in the My Computer window.

This step ensures a consistent starting place for the lesson.

2 Click File on the My Computer menu bar.

Clicking a menu name opens the menu, which cascades down from the menu bar (thus, the term *pull-down menu* is used to describe Windows menus). In this case, the **F**ile menu cascades down from the menu bar into the screen, and a list of commands appears (see Figure 1.6).

The underlined letter, in this case, the "F" in "File" is called a *hot key*. In this book, hot keys are shown in a different color for clarity.

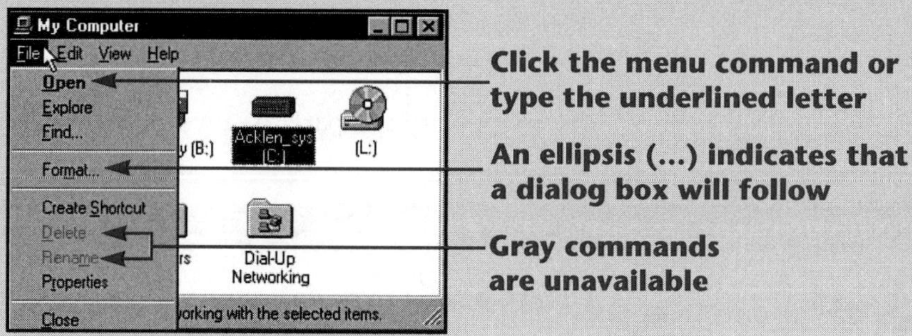

Figure 1.6
Clicking **F**ile on the menu bar pulls down the **F**ile menu.

An ellipsis (...) after a command tells you that a dialog box appears when you select the command. (You learn more about dialog boxes in the next lesson.) A right-facing triangle indicates that a submenu will appear. If a menu command is gray, it is currently unavailable. This means that you need to do something, such as select text, before you can use the command. In Figure 1.6, the **D**elete and Rena**m**e commands are gray.

If you have problems...

If the options on your **F**ile menu do not match the ones shown in Figure 1.6, it's probably because you have a different icon selected (the drive C: icon is selected in Figure 1.6). Windows menus change, depending on what is currently selected. Click the drive C: icon; then open the **F**ile menu again.

3 In the File menu, click Properties.

This step opens the Properties dialog box, which displays the amount of free space and used space on the selected drive (see Figure 1.7).

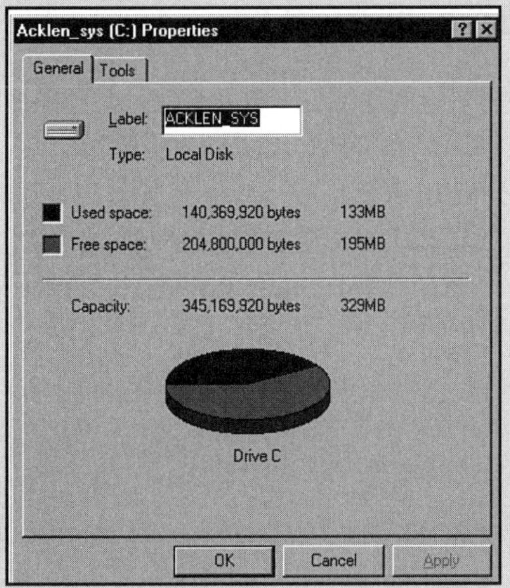

Figure 1.7
The Properties dialog box appears after you choose Properties from the **F**ile menu.

4 Click the Cancel button.

Clicking the Cancel button closes the Properties dialog box.

You can also use the keyboard to open and make selections from menus in Windows. To open a menu with the keyboard, press Alt and then type the underlined letter. If you prefer, you can also hold down Alt while you press the underlined letter.

Use keyboard techniques to open and select from the **F**ile menu now.

5 Press Alt + F.

Pressing Alt+F opens the **F**ile menu. After the menu is open, you just press the underlined letter for the menu command (without Alt) to choose a menu command.

6 Press R.

Pressing R chooses the P**r**operties command, which opens the Properties dialog box.

7 Press Esc.

This cancels the dialog box.

continued

8 Press Alt+F again.

Selection bar
A dark background or border that appears around selected area in a window

You can also use the arrow keys and press ↵Enter to choose menu commands. When a menu is displayed, use ↑ and ↓ to move a *selection bar* through the menu commands on that menu; use ← and → to move the selection bar across to another menu.

9 Press ↓ several times.

This moves the selection bar down through the menu commands on the **F**ile menu. When a command is highlighted, you can press ↵Enter to select the command.

10 Press → twice.

Pressing → twice moves through the pull-down menus to the **V**iew pull-down menu, which is two menus to the right of the **F**ile menu. The **V**iew menu opens and the **F**ile menu closes, as shown in Figure 1.8. A check mark (or dot) next to a menu command indicates that the command is currently selected, or turned on. In this case, the check mark next to the Status **B**ar option tells you that the status bar is currently displayed.

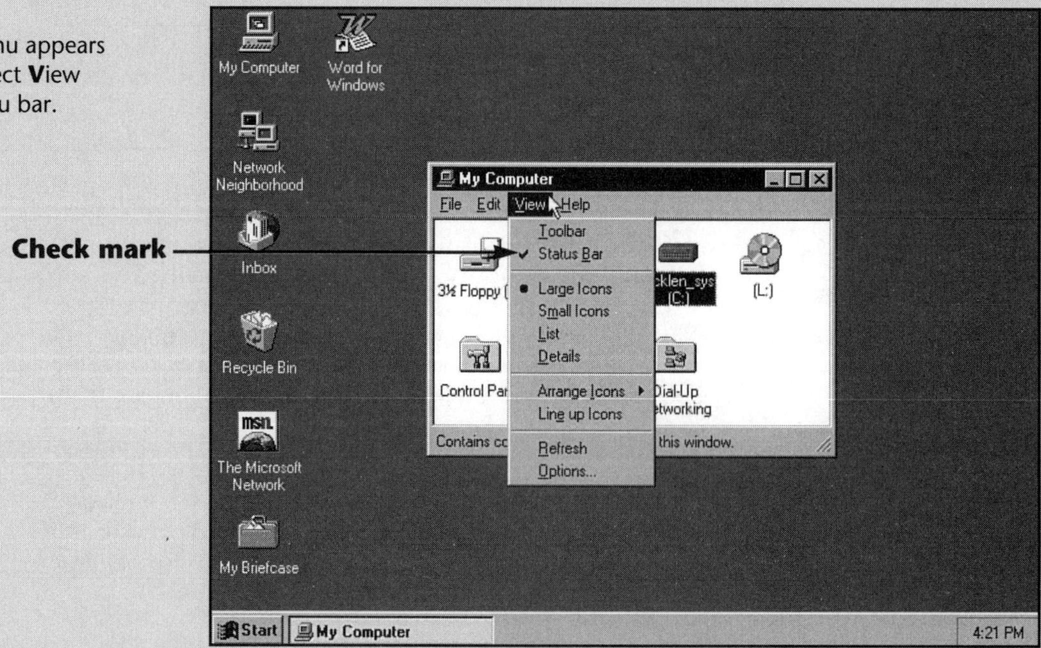

Figure 1.8
The **V**iew menu appears when you select **V**iew from the menu bar.

11 Press Esc twice.

This action cancels a menu without making any selections. In this case, the **V**iew menu disappears. Here again, you can cancel a menu if you change your mind or find that you opened the wrong menu.

You should now be familiar with the use of the menu bar. In this lesson, you learned how to make selections in the My Computer menus, so you now know how to make selections in any Windows application menu because all Windows programs operate the same way. In the next lesson, you learn how to make selections in dialog boxes.

Lesson 5: Using Dialog Boxes

Some commands need additional information before the computer can execute the commands you have chosen. In the pull-down menus, an ellipsis (...) after a menu command means that a dialog box appears so you can enter the necessary information to complete the command.

Besides including many windows options, such as the Close button and the Control-menu box, dialog boxes contain different items designed to help you enter data or select options for a command. Table 1.2 lists these items and summarizes their uses. Refer to the following figures for examples of dialog box elements.

Table 1.2 Dialog Box Elements

Element	Description
Tab	A button that resembles a file folder tab and is located on the top of a dialog box. Clicking a tab switches to and displays a different page for the dialog box.
Text box	A data entry area for text, data, or numbers.
List box	A list of predefined data entry items, options, or existing files or directories. If a scroll bar is present, there are more entries than will show in the list.
Drop-down list box	A list box that conserves space on the screen by not displaying the entire list until you click the arrow button next to the box. A full list of options drops down so you can choose an item.
Command button	A large rectangular button that executes or cancels a dialog box. A command button displaying an ellipsis opens another dialog box.
Check box	A square box that specifies an option. You can select more than one check box; a check mark in the check box indicates that the option is selected.
Option button	A round button that specifies an option. An option button is also referred to as a radio button. You can select only one button from a group; the selected button is filled with a dark circle.

Both the Windows program and all programs designed for Windows use dialog boxes, so it's important that you learn how to use all the elements correctly. After a little practice, you will see how dialog boxes enable you to make selections faster and more easily. Open a couple of dialog boxes and practice making selections now.

To Use Dialog Boxes

1 Click File on the menu bar.

Clicking **F**ile on the menu bar opens the **F**ile menu. In the preceding lesson, you learned how to use the mouse and the keyboard to open and select from menus. Because Windows is designed to be used with a mouse, and the mouse technique is often the fastest method, the lessons in this book emphasize the mouse technique. Shortcut keys and other keyboard techniques are mentioned in the Inside Stuff sections.

2 Click the Find command.

Clicking **F**ind opens the Find dialog box (see Figure 1.9). You use this dialog box to search for files. Three tabs are at the top of the dialog box: Name & Location, Date Modified, and Advanced. The first tab is selected (it's in front of the others), so this is the Name & Location page of the Find dialog box.

Figure 1.9
The Find dialog box appears when you click the **F**ind command.

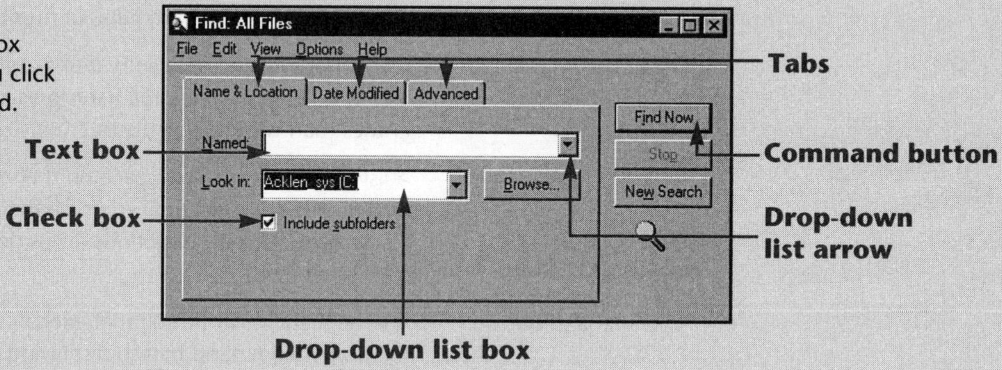

Insertion point
A blinking vertical line in Windows applications that marks the location on-screen where the next character you type will appear.

The Find dialog box has a text box, a drop-down list arrow, a drop-down list box, a command button, and a check box. The *insertion point*, which indicates where the text you type will be placed, is already positioned in the text box. As soon as the dialog box appears, you can start typing the name of the file you want to find.

3 Type Que.bmp.

This is the name of the file you want to search for.

4 Click the drop-down list arrow to the right of the Look In list box.

Clicking the drop-down list arrow opens a list of the drives available on your system (where you can look for a file). To switch to another drive, click the drive letter in the list, or use My Computer to select a drive not listed.

5 Click in the dialog box.

Alternatively, press Esc. This step closes the drop-down list (without making a selection).

6 Click the Include Subfolders check box.

When a check mark appears in the check box, the item is selected, or turned on. Clicking the check box again removes the check mark and deselects, or turns off, the option.

7 Click the Browse command button.

Clicking the **B**rowse command button opens the Browse for Folder dialog box (see Figure 1.10). You use this type of dialog box to look for files when you can't remember the exact name or location.

Figure 1.10
In the Browse for Folder dialog box, you select a folder where you want to begin a search for a file.

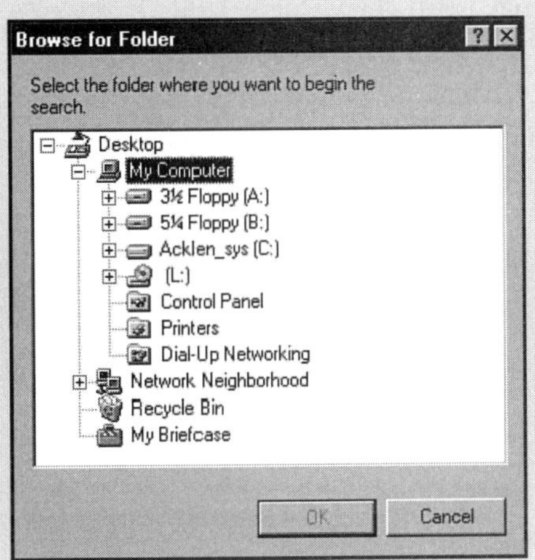

8 Click a floppy drive icon in the list.

Depending on your system, you will have a floppy drive icon for drive A or B, or both. Clicking this icon selects the floppy drive where you want to start searching for the file.

9 Click the OK command button.

Clicking OK closes the Browse for Folder dialog box and saves the selection you made there. If you click the Cancel button, you cancel the dialog box without saving your selection. Notice that the name of the floppy drive now appears in the **L**ook In list box (see Figure 1.11).

Figure 1.11
The selected floppy drive name appears in the **L**ook In list box of the Find dialog box.

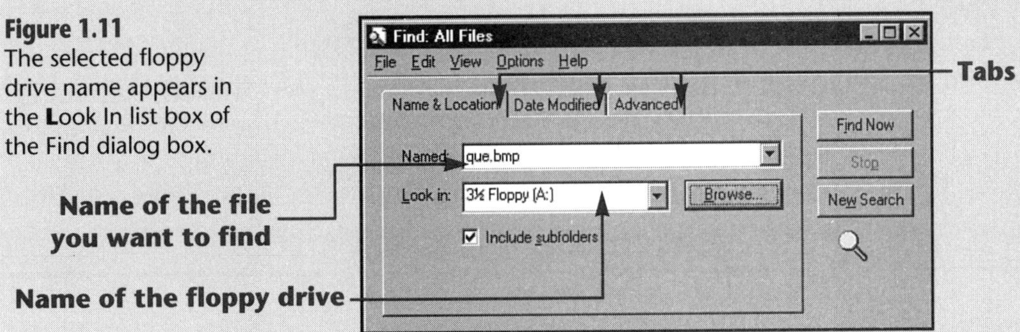

continues

To Use Dialog Boxes (continued)

As noted, clicking the tabs to the right of the Name & Location tab switch you to other pages in the dialog box. Switch to another page now.

10 Click the Date Modified tab below the menu bar of the Find dialog box.

Clicking the Date Modified tab switches you to the Date Modified page where you can search for a file based on the date it was created or modified (see Figure 1.12). This dialog box has a series of option buttons.

Notice how the selected tab moves to the front and the tab name has a dotted line surrounding it.

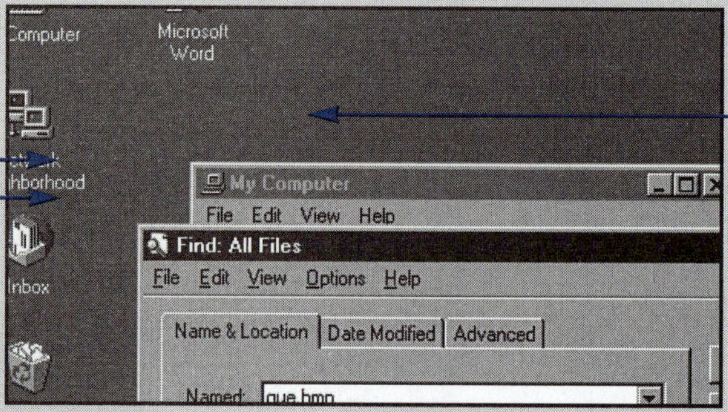

Figure 1.12
You use the Date Modified page to search for a file by the date it was created or modified.

11 Click the Find all files created or modified option button.

Clicking this option button selects the option. (The empty circle turns into a filled circle, which means that the item is currently selected.) You can only select one option button at a time, so when you choose Find all files created or **m**odified, the **A**ll files option is deselected, or turned off.

12 Click each of the three option buttons under Find all files created or modified.

Clicking an option button makes it the active option. Because you can select only one option button in a series, the other two options are grayed, indicating that they are not available.

13 Click the Close button (on the title bar).

Clicking the Close button closes the dialog box without performing an action. Because you are just practicing in this lesson, you won't actually search for a file. You will have plenty of opportunities to use dialog box options as you work through the projects in this book.

If the insertion point isn't already in a text box, just click the text box to place the insertion point inside it. If you need to correct mistakes in a text box, position the mouse pointer where you need to make the correction, and click once. Press Backspace to delete one character to the left, or press Del to remove one character to the right.

In step 5, you used the mouse to click the check box. You can also click the check box name to select or deselect the check box. Likewise, in step 12, you used the mouse to click the option button itself, but you can also click the option name (for example, **B**etween) to select or deselect the option button.

Remember the primary difference between check boxes and option buttons. In a series of check boxes, you can select one or more check boxes at one time; in a series of option buttons, you can select only one option button at a time.

Lesson 6: Using the Help System

Online
A built-in feature of a program, such as an online Help system.

One reason why Windows applications are so easy to use is because they offer users an extensive Help feature. The Help feature is *online*, so it's easy to get help on any area of the program without having to search through software manuals. A special What's This? option allows you to click in the area of the dialog box where you want help. Shortcut buttons in some help topics take you directly to the area in the program where you need to make your changes.

Windows help topics are fairly brief, with more emphasis on step-by-step instructions and less emphasis on explanatory text. You can even print help topics if you want to refer to them later.

To Use the Help System

1. **In the My Computer window, click Help on the menu bar.**

   Clicking **H**elp opens the **H**elp menu.

2. **Choose Help Topics.**

   This opens the Help Topics dialog box (see Figure 1.13), where you can search through the entire Windows Help system. There are three ways to locate help topics in Windows Help: through the Contents topics, the Index list, or a search by key words.

3. **Click the Contents tab.**

   Clicking the Contents tab switches to the Contents page. (This step may not be necessary if the Contents page is already displayed.) The Contents page presents help topics organized by category. Each category is represented by a book icon (see Figure 1.13). The Contents view is helpful if you know the area of the program where you need help, but not the specific name of the feature.

continues

To Use the Help System (continued)

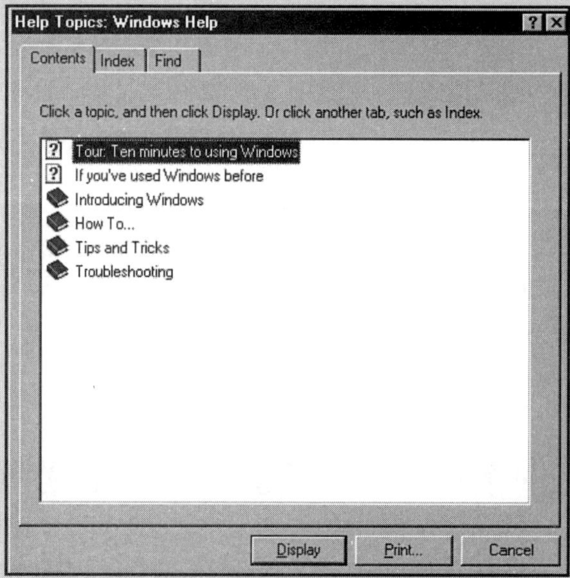

Figure 1.13
The Help Topics dialog box appears after you choose **H**elp Topics from the **H**elp menu.

4 Double-click the How To book icon.

Double-clicking the How To book icon shows you what topics are in the How To category (see Figure 1.14). When you open a category, the icon changes to an open book.

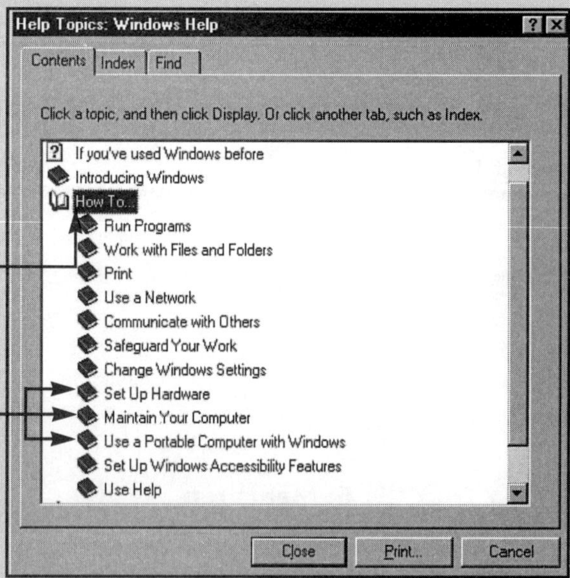

Figure 1.14
The open book icon appears after you double-click the How To book icon on the Contents page.

Open categories are represented by open book icons

Categories are represented by book icons

5 Double-click the Run Programs book icon.

Double-clicking this icon displays a list of topics in that category (see Figure 1.15). The topics are represented by page icons.

Figure 1.15
The topics in the Run Programs category.

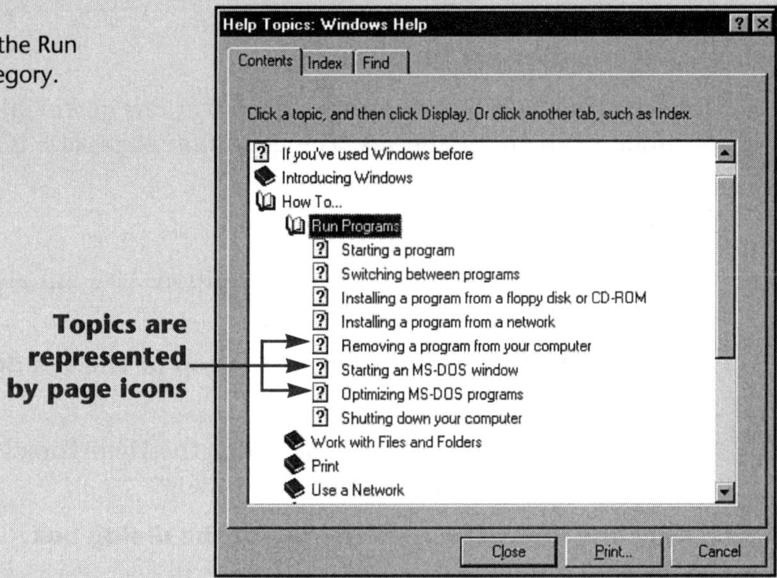

6 Double-click the Starting a Program page icon.

Double-clicking this page icon opens the Windows Help window and displays the help information for starting a program (see Figure 1.16). Use the scroll bar to scroll down to the bottom of the help topic.

Some help topics have a glossary term shown in green with a dotted underline. When you point to a glossary term, the mouse pointer changes to a pointing hand.

Figure 1.16
This is a page of help information for starting a program that contains a glossary term.

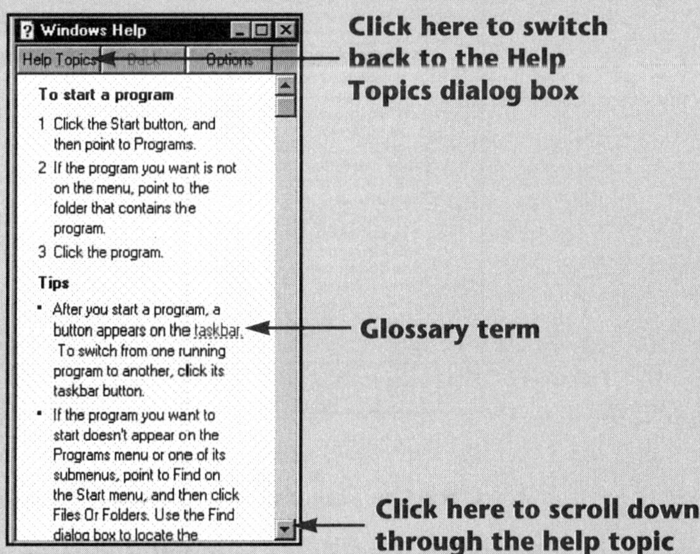

continues

To Use the Help System (continued)

7 **Click the glossary term `taskbar`.**

Clicking a glossary term opens a small window in which a short definition of the term appears. The definition of `taskbar` is now in the window.

8 **Click in the Help window.**

This step clears the glossary term definition. You can also press Esc to clear the definition, if you like.

9 **Click the Help Topics button at the top of the Windows Help window.**

Clicking the Help **T**opics button opens the Help Topics dialog box again. It appears on top of the Help window.

10 **Click the Index tab near the top of the dialog box.**

Clicking the Index tab switches to the Index page where you can search through an index of help topics.

11 **Type date.**

As you type the word **date**, Windows searches through the index for a match (see Figure 1.17).

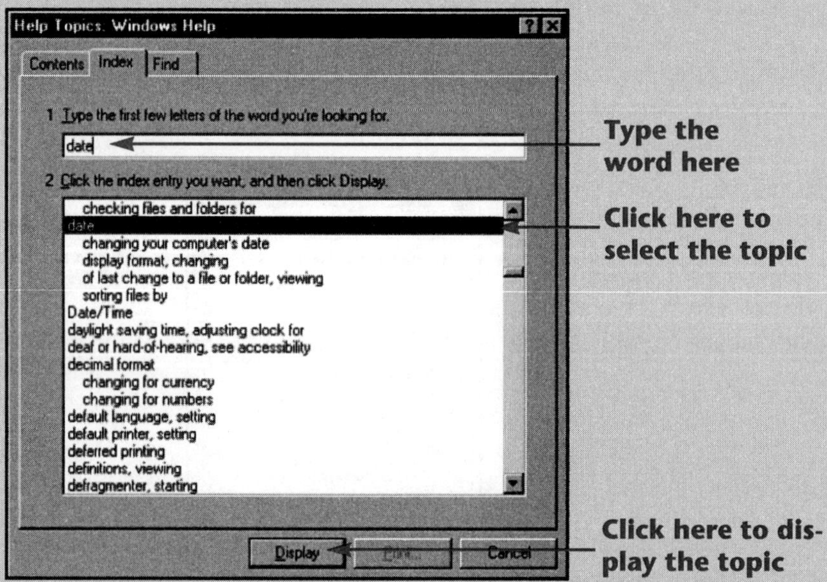

Figure 1.17
You type a term on the Index page to search for a topic.

12 **Click the `changing your computer's date` help topic in the list.**

13 **Click the Display command button.**

The Help window opens, and the selected help topic appears (see Figure 1.18). This help topic includes a shortcut button to take you to the area of the program where you can change the computer's date.

Figure 1.18
This is the Help window for the help topic of changing your computer's date.

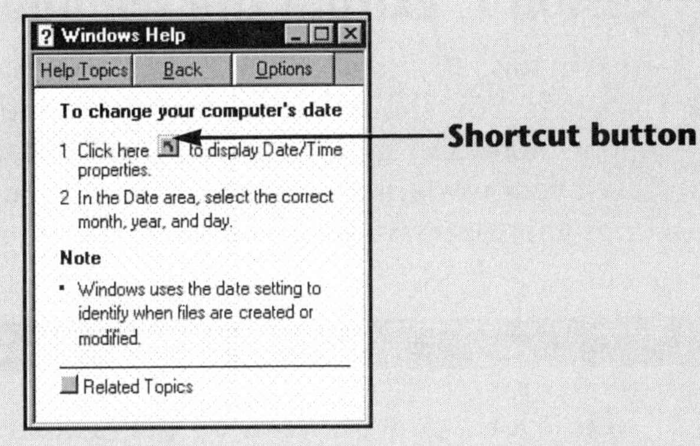

14 Click the Shortcut button.

Clicking the Shortcut button takes you to the Date/Time Properties dialog box, where you can change the system date and time. (See Lesson 3 in Project 6 for more information on changing the system date and time.)

Because you are just practicing with the Help system, close the dialog box for now.

15 Click Cancel.

This closes the Date/Time Properties dialog box. The Windows Help dialog box is the active dialog box now.

16 Click the Close button.

The Help window closes. Now that you have some experience using the Help system, make a point of using it the next time you have a question about the program. The more you use it, the more you realize how easy it is to use. Remember, every Windows application has a Help system similar to this one.

The Find page of the Help Topics dialog box enables you to search for specific words and phrases in help topics, instead of searching for information by category. Click the Find tab to switch to the Find page of the Help Topics dialog box. Type **games** in the Type the Word You Want to Find text box. Windows displays Help topics that contain that word in the Click a Topic, Then Click Display list box. Select the Accessories Playing Windows Games check box; then click **D**isplay to display that help topic.

A Related Topics button appears at the bottom of many help screens. Clicking this button displays a list of topics related to the current help topic. You can jump to another help topic by selecting one from this list.

The What's This? option is available in many areas of the Windows program. In some cases, a question mark button appears in the title bar; in others, a What's This? option appears on the **H**elp menu. Either click the question mark icon or select the What's This? option on the **H**elp menu to change the mouse pointer to a pointer with a question mark. Click any area of the current window or dialog box to display a short description of the item. Click in the description or in the dialog box to close the description and turn off the What's This? option.

Lesson 7: Exiting the Windows Program

In Windows 95, you use the Shut Down command to exit the Windows program. You should always use this command, which closes all open applications and files, before you turn off the computer. If you haven't saved your work in an application when you choose this command, you'll be prompted to save your changes before Windows shuts down.

To Exit Windows

1 Click the Start button on the taskbar.

Clicking the Start button opens the Start menu. (Project 2 discusses the Start menu in "Lesson 1: Starting Applications.")

2 Choose Shut Down.

The Shut Down Windows dialog box appears (see Figure 1.19).

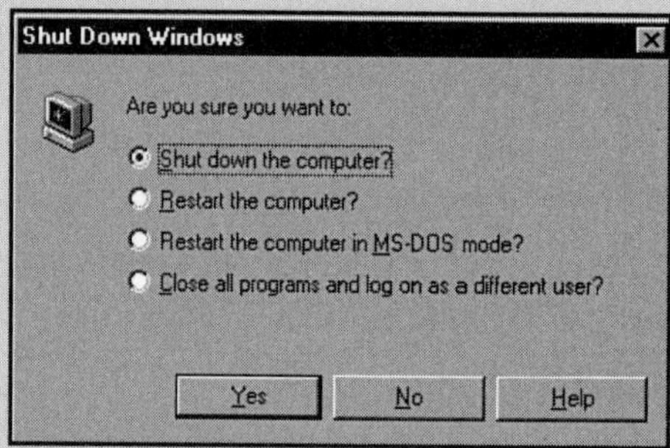

Figure 1.19
The Shut Down Windows dialog box appears after you choose Shut Down from the Start menu.

3 Choose Shut down the computer.

This option closes all the active applications and files.

4 Choose Yes.

Windows displays a message asking you to wait while the computer is shutting down. When this process is complete, a message appears telling you that you can safely turn off your computer now.

If you would like to continue with the next section, "Applying Your Skills," restart your computer.

Summary

To...	Do This
Start Windows	Turn on your computer and your monitor. Type **win** at the DOS prompt.
Move the mouse pointer	Slide the mouse across your desk or mouse pad.
Click	Press and release the left mouse button.

Double-click	Press and release the left mouse button twice in rapid succession.
Right-click	Press and release the right mouse button.
Drag and drop	Point to an object. Press and hold down the left mouse button while moving the mouse to a different location. Release the left mouse button to "drop" the object.
Open a menu	Click the menu name in the menu bar, or press Alt, then the underlined letter in the menu name.
Choose a menu command	Click the menu command, or press Alt, then the underlined letter in the menu command.
Select a text box	Click the text box.
Select text in a text box	Double-click the text box.
Make a selection from a drop-down list	Click the underlined arrow beside the list, then click an item in the list. If necessary, click the up or down arrow in the scroll bar to scroll through the list.
Select (or deselect) a check box	Click the check box or the item name.
Select a command button	Click the command button.
Make a selection from a list box	Click the item in the list. If necessary, click the up or down scroll arrow to scroll through the list.
Switch to a different page	Click the tab along the top of the dialog box.
Select an option button	Click the option button or the item name.
Cancel a dialog box	Click the Cancel command button or press Esc.
Get help from the desktop	Click the Start button, then choose **H**elp.
Get help in an application	Click **H**elp on the menu bar, then choose **H**elp Topics.
Display the Help Contents page	Click the Contents tab in the Help Topics dialog box.
Display the Help Index page	Click the Index tab in the Help Topics dialog box.
Search for a help topic	In the Index page, type the first few letters of the help topic you want to find. Click the help topic in the list box, then choose **D**isplay.
Perform a word search on help topics	Click the Find tab in the Help Topics dialog box. Type the word you want to find in the help topics in the **T**ype the Word(s) You Want To Find text box. If necessary, choose the matching word in the **S**elect Some Matching Words To Narrow Your Search list box. Select a help topic in the **C**lick a Topic, Then Click Display list box, then choose **D**isplay.
Exit Windows	Click the Start button, then choose Sh**u**t Down. Choose **S**hut Down the Computer, then choose **Y**es. It's okay to turn the computer off when the message `It's now safe to turn off your computer` appears.

Applying Your Skills

These "On Your Own" exercises enable you to practice the skills you have learned in this project. Take a few minutes to work through these exercises now.

On Your Own

Becoming Familiar with Windows 95 Window Elements

For each term in the left column, define its purpose in the right column.

Window Element	Definition
Minimize button	
Maximize button	
Title bar	
Menu bar	
Window border	
Window corner	
Close button	

Becoming Familiar with Windows 95 Help

1. Using the **H**elp command, run the 10-minute tour of Windows 95. Complete all five sections of the tour.
2. Double-click the Introducing Windows book icon. Double-click the Welcome book icon. Double-click the A List of What's New book icon. Double-click the A New Look and Feel page icon to display a list of new features and enhancements in the Windows 95 program. Click each of the 11 buttons to display a short description of each item in the What's New window. Then close the What's New window.
3. Click the Help **T**opics button to switch back to the Help Topics window. Click the Index tab at the top of the Help Topics window to switch to the Index page. Search for the following help topics:
   a. *Skills, Basic*. Choose **D**isplay to open the Basic Skills help topic. Click each of the six buttons to review basic skills. Click the Help **T**opics button to switch to the Help Topics window.
   b. *Accessories*. Display the help topic titled `about new accessories`. Click several of the accessory buttons to display a brief description of that accessory program in the What's New window.

Becoming Familiar with the Mouse

1. Place the mouse pointer on the taskbar and click the *right* mouse button. A Context menu for the taskbar appears.

2. Move the mouse pointer up into the desktop and click the left mouse button. This clears the Context menu without choosing any of the commands.
3. Click the Recycle Bin to select it. Notice that the icon appears highlighted, indicating that it has been chosen.
4. Double-click the Recycle Bin icon to open it in a window. Close the window by clicking the Close button (X) located in the upper-right corner of the window.
5. Place the mouse pointer on the Recycle Bin icon and right-click to bring up the Context menu. Notice that the options displayed are related to the Recycle Bin. Click the left mouse button on the Open command. The Recycle Bin opens in a window just as it did when you double-clicked it. Close the window.
6. Rearrange the icons located on your desktop by dragging and dropping them into different locations.
7. Drag the icons back to their original locations.

Working with Menus and Dialog Boxes

1. Double-click the My Computer icon to open My Computer.
2. Using your mouse, click **H**elp, **H**elp Topics. This activates the Help dialog box on the screen. Click the Cancel button (located at the bottom of the dialog box) to clear the dialog box.
3. Now try the same menu sequence by using the keyboard. Press Alt+H to activate the **H**elp menu. After the menu appears, simply press H to choose **H**elp Topics. To clear the dialog box, press Esc
4. Click the **V**iew menu.
5. To clear the pull-down menu without making any selections, press Esc twice.
6. Choose **V**iew, **O**ptions by using the mouse or the keyboard (whichever you prefer). Notice that **O**ptions is followed by an ellipsis (...), indicating that a dialog box will result.
7. Click the tabs near the top of the dialog box to bring up related "pages" of information: Folder, View, File Types.
8. Select the Folder tab. Notice that two option buttons are available in the Browsing options section. When you select one of these buttons (by clicking it), the other button is automatically deselected.
9. Select the View tab. Both check boxes and option buttons are present. Click each of the option buttons, again noting that selecting one deselects the other. Then practice clicking the check boxes. Notice that the check boxes differ from the option buttons in that you can choose neither check box, just one, or both.
10. Click the Cancel button when you are finished making choices to negate any options you chose.

Project 2

Running Applications

Objectives

In this project, you learn how to

- Start Applications
- Switch between Applications
- Arrange Application Windows
- Maximize, Minimize, and Restore a Window
- Close an Application Window

Why Would I Do This?

Most of us work in more than one application at a time. One of the advantages of Windows is that it enables you to start and run multiple applications at the same time. The capability to switch between applications increases productivity and facilitates the sharing of information between applications. For example, you might be writing a financial report in a word processor, referencing year-end figures in a spreadsheet program, and looking up dates in a calendar program. You can switch among all three applications and even copy information from one to another.

When you start an application in Windows, that application opens in a window. You can size an application window to take up the whole screen or part of the screen. It's very easy to size and arrange application windows so you can see the contents of several application windows (document, spreadsheet, and calendar, for example) at the same time.

If you are just getting started in Windows, or if you have been using Windows but have never worked with more than one application at a time, this project shows you how to start an application and switch among multiple applications. You also learn how to arrange application windows and then close them. Finally, you learn how to minimize, maximize, and restore windows.

Lesson 1: Starting Applications

In Windows 95, you use the Start button on the taskbar to start applications. Choosing the **P**rograms option at the top of the Start menu displays the Programs menu, which lists the *applications* you have installed on your system (see Figure 2.1). *Program folders* are listed first, followed by *shortcuts*.

Figure 2.1
Click the Start button to open the Start menu.

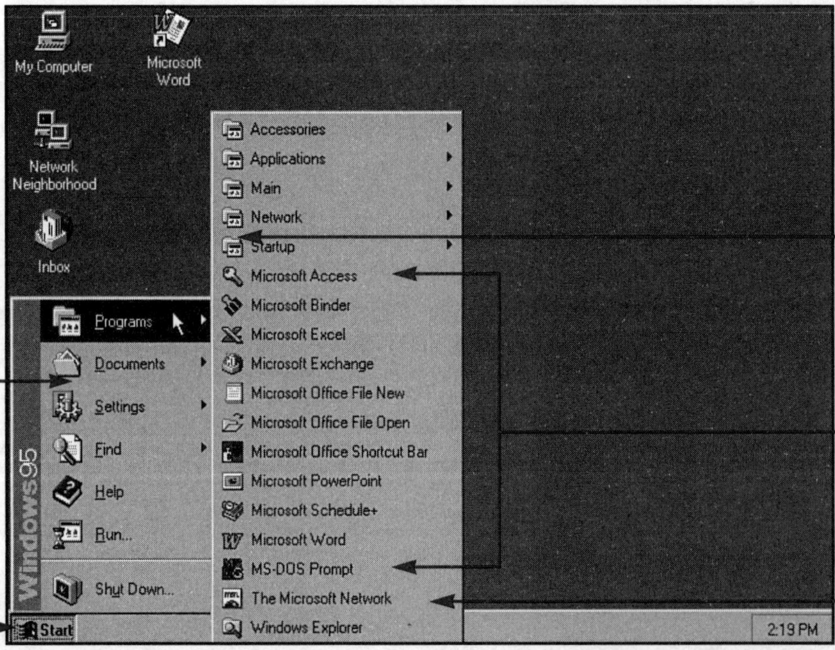

A program folder is represented by an icon of a file folder with an application window in front of it so you get the idea that applications are in that folder. Windows and applications designed for Windows create their own program folders when they are installed. For example, the Accessories folder, which contains icons for all the Windows Accessories programs, is created when you install Windows.

The *icons* at the bottom of the Programs menu are shortcuts. They give you quick access to items that are ordinarily out of sight. For example, you can create a shortcut to a program that would normally require navigating through several program folders to find. The shortcuts shown in Figure 2.1 were created during the Windows installation.

Jargon Watch

The terms **application** and **program** are interchangeable. Both refer to computer programs, like WordPerfect or Excel, which are instructions that tell the computer how to operate and what to do when you choose a command.

A **program folder** can contain shortcuts and other program folders. Shortcuts to related programs are grouped together in a program folder. You can create subfolders within folders to organize your programs, using the same concepts as your paper filing system. For example, the Accessories folder contains the Games folder.

A **shortcut** gives you quick access to frequently used objects so you don't have to look through the menus each time you need to use that object. An **icon** is a picture that represents an application, a file, or a system resource.

To Start Applications

1 Click the Start button.

Clicking the Start button opens the Start menu (refer to Figure 2.1). A right-pointing triangle to the right of a menu option (such as **P**rograms, **D**ocuments, **S**ettings, and **F**ind) indicates that another menu will open when you select that item.

2 Move the mouse pointer up the menu to highlight Programs.

Moving the mouse pointer moves a selection bar through the options on the Start menu. When you highlight **P**rograms, a list of program folders and shortcuts appears (see Figure 2.2).

continues

To Start Applications (continued)

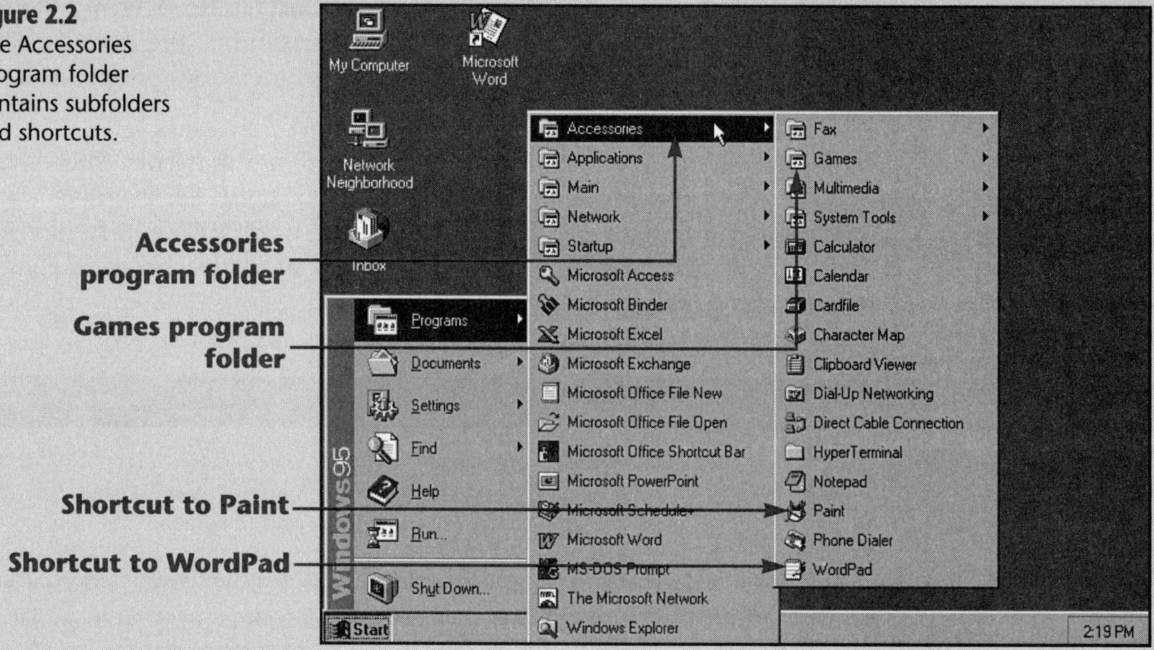

Figure 2.2
The Accessories program folder contains subfolders and shortcuts.

3 Move the mouse pointer to the right to place the selection bar on the Accessories program folder.

Moving the selection bar to a program folder opens a pop-up list of its contents. When you point to the Accessories program folder, a list of program folders and shortcuts appears (refer to Figure 2.2). The Games program folder is a subfolder of the Accessories program folder.

4 Move the mouse pointer to the Paint option; then click the left mouse button.

Clicking a shortcut icon starts the file the shortcut points to. In this case, clicking the icon starts the Paint program, which opens in a window on the desktop (see Figure 2.3). A button for the Paint program appears on the taskbar.

The Start menu is always available so you can start another program now.

If you have problems...

If you have problems selecting from the Accessories menu, make sure that you move the mouse all the way to the right until you are pointing inside the Accessories menu *before* you move the mouse up or down to select a shortcut. The mouse has to be all the way inside the menu you want to move around in.

❺ Click the Start button; then move the mouse up to highlight Programs.

Figure 2.3
You use the Paint program to create and edit bitmap files.

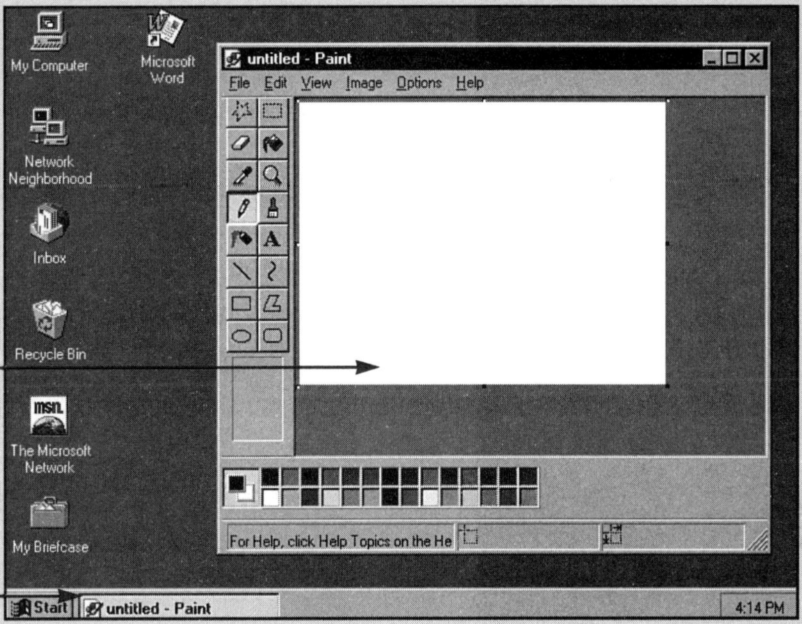

❻ Highlight Accessories; then click the WordPad shortcut icon.

Clicking the icon opens the WordPad program in a window in front of the Paint window on the desktop (see Figure 2.4). A button for the WordPad program appears on the taskbar.

Two buttons are now on the taskbar: Paint and WordPad. (The word `untitled` next to the Paint program name means you have not named the file in the Paint program yet.) You currently have two applications—Paint and WordPad—running at the same time. Leave these applications running for the next lesson.

Figure 2.4
You use the WordPad program to create and edit documents.

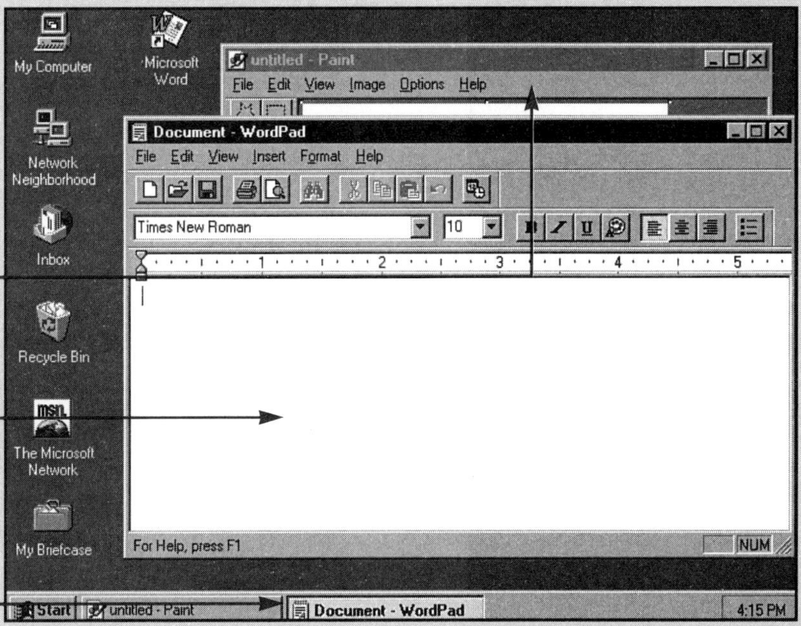

Depending on your computer's setup, your menus and folders might differ slightly from that shown in the figures.

In Figure 2.2, the Accessories program folder is open to reveal a series of other program folders (such as Fax, Games, Multimedia, and System Tools). These other program folders are called *subfolders* because they are inside another folder. This system of organizing programs (and files) is similar to the traditional paper filing system that uses file cabinets, hanging folders, and manila folders.

You can also start applications by selecting a document from the **D**ocuments menu. The **D**ocuments option on the Start menu opens a list of the last 15 documents you opened. Selecting a document from this list automatically launches the appropriate application and opens the file.

Lesson 2: Switching between Applications

Windows makes it very easy to switch between open applications. There are several methods to choose from, so this lesson introduces you to each method. The fastest way to switch to a different program is to click the program button on the taskbar. If you prefer to use the keyboard, you can use shortcut keys to switch between programs. Finally, you can click anywhere in the application window to make that the active window, which moves it to the front of the stack.

Now that two applications windows are open on the desktop, you are ready to learn how to switch between these programs.

To Switch between Applications

1. **Click the Paint button on the taskbar.**

   Clicking the Paint button moves the Paint window in front of the WordPad window (see Figure 2.5). The Paint window is now the "active" window. Notice that the title bar in the Paint window is blue and the title bar in the WordPad window is gray. Blue indicates the active window; gray indicates an inactive window.

   The Paint button on the taskbar now looks as if it has been pressed down. This effect graphically shows you which button is currently selected.

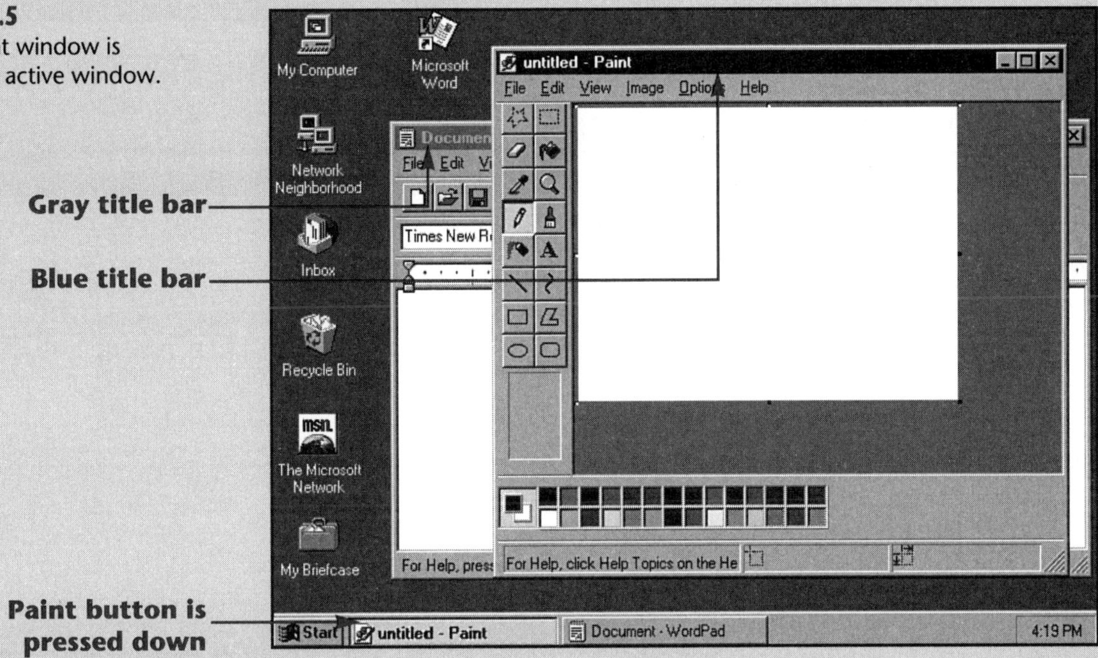

Figure 2.5
The Paint window is now the active window.

❷ **Click the WordPad button on the taskbar.**

Clicking the WordPad button moves the WordPad window in front of the Paint window.

If your hands are already on the keyboard and you don't want to use the mouse, you can switch to another program with a couple of shortcut keys. Try using the shortcut keys now.

❸ **Press Alt+Esc.**

Pressing this key combination switches to the Paint window. This keyboard shortcut cycles through the open application windows, one by one. The active window moves to the front, and the title bar appears in blue.

❹ **Press and hold down Alt, then tap Tab.**

Pressing and holding down Alt, then pressing Tab opens a small window in the middle of the screen (see Figure 2.6). Icons for the applications are shown; the active application's icon has a blue box around it. The window displays the name of the open (or active) application.

continues

To Switch between Applications (continued)

Figure 2.6
Pressing Alt+Tab opens a small window in the middle of the screen.

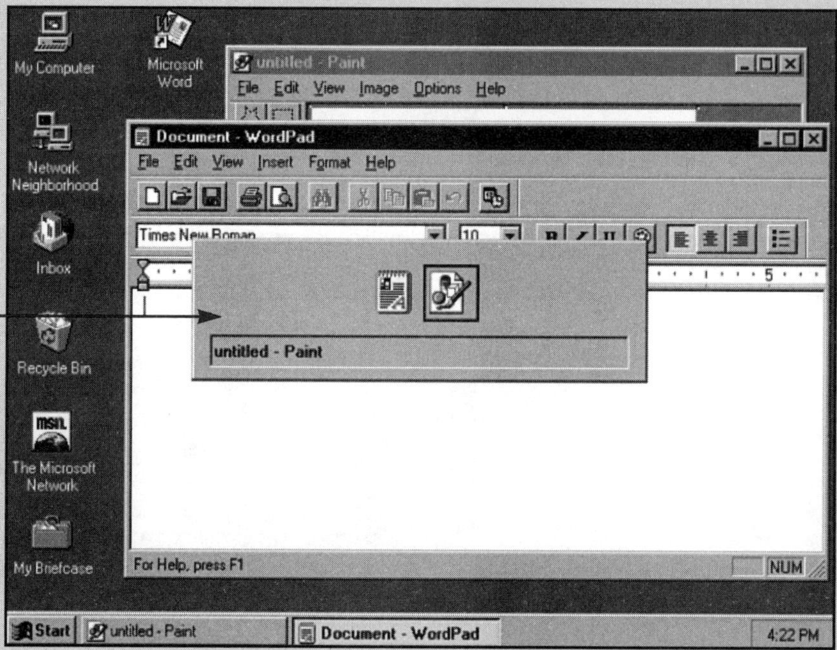

If you have problems...

You have to keep holding down the Alt key or the window will disappear. Press and hold the Altt key, then tap the Tab key. Don't release the Alt key until you select the program you want to switch to (see the next step).

5 While still holding down Alt, press Tab a couple of times.

Pressing Tab moves the blue box from icon to icon. When the box encloses the icon for the program you want, release Alt.

6 When the WordPad icon is selected, release Alt.

The WordPad window moves in front of the Paint window. Now try the last method—clicking in an application window to switch to it.

7 Click the Paint window.

Clicking inside the Paint window switches to it. You can click in the window, the title bar, the menu bar, inside the editing area, and so on, to switch to that application.

8 Click the WordPad window.

The WordPad window is now the active window, so it should be in front of the Paint window. Leave the desktop in this state for the next lesson.

INSIDE Stuff

Because you worked with only two open applications in this lesson, the taskbar didn't get too crowded. If you have quite a few applications open, however, the buttons on the taskbar can get too small to read. If this happens, consider resizing the taskbar. Position the mouse pointer over the top border of the taskbar. The mouse pointer changes to a double-headed arrow. Click and drag up to increase the size of the taskbar. Release the mouse button when you are done.

Lesson 3: Arranging Application Windows

Changing the size and position of a window enables you to see more than one application window, which makes copying and pasting data between programs much easier. You can also move a window to any location on the desktop. By moving application windows, you can arrange your work on the Windows desktop just as you arrange papers on your desk.

In this lesson, you learn how to change the size and position of windows on the desktop. You can do this manually by clicking and dragging with the mouse, or you can use commands from the taskbar.

Now try to size and move windows manually on the desktop.

To Size and Move Windows Manually

1 Move the mouse pointer to the border on the left side of the WordPad window.

When the mouse pointer is correctly positioned, it changes to a two-headed arrow (see Figure 2.7).

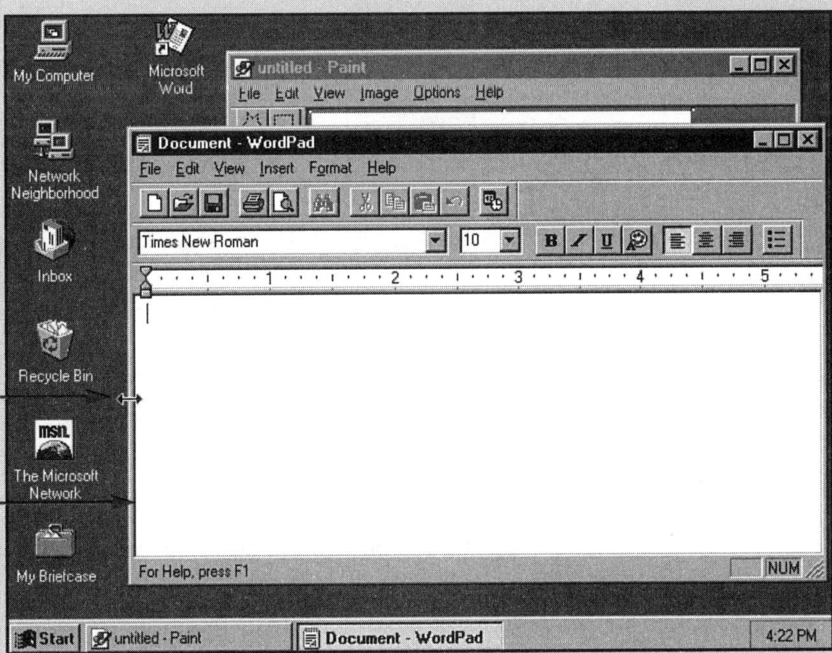

Two-headed arrow

Window border

Figure 2.7
The mouse pointer becomes a two headed arrow.

continues

To Size and Move Windows Manually (continued)

The two-headed arrow indicates the directions in which you can size a window. If you click and drag a side border, you can size the window to the left or the right. If you start on a top or bottom border, you can size the window up or down.

If you have problems...

If you don't see a two-headed arrow, make sure you move the pointer back and forth over the border *slowly*.

2 Move the two-headed arrow to the left to make the window wider.

When you drag a window border, an outline of the border appears as a guide so you can see how large or small the window will be when you release the mouse button (see Figure 2.8).

Figure 2.8
The red outline acts as a sizing guide.

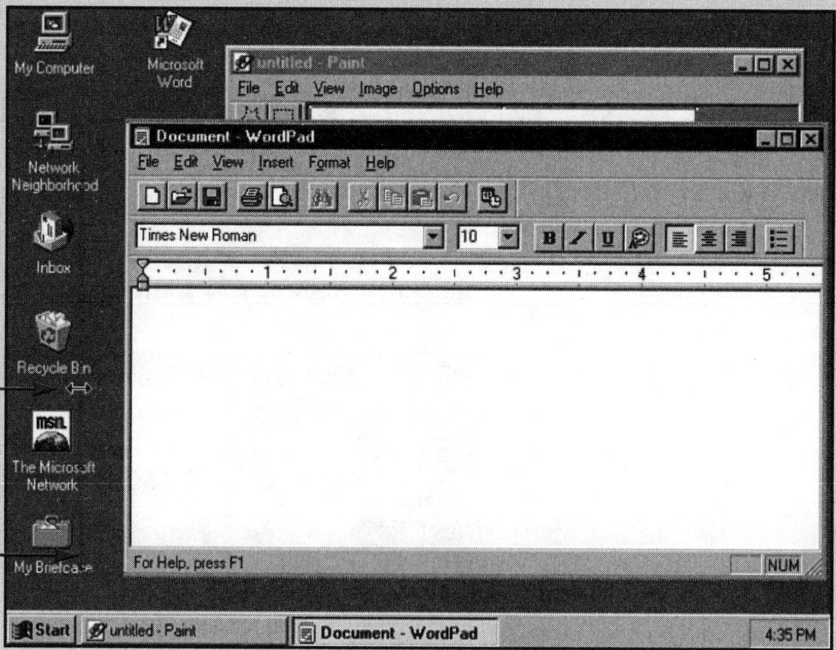

3 Move the two-headed mouse pointer to the right and then release the mouse button.

This action makes the window smaller. When you release the mouse button, Windows resizes the window to the new dimensions.

4 Place the mouse pointer on the upper-left corner of the window.

The mouse pointer changes to a diagonal two-headed arrow (see Figure 2.9).

Figure 2.9
Pointing to a window corner changes the mouse pointer to a diagonal two-headed arrow.

Diagonal two-headed arrow

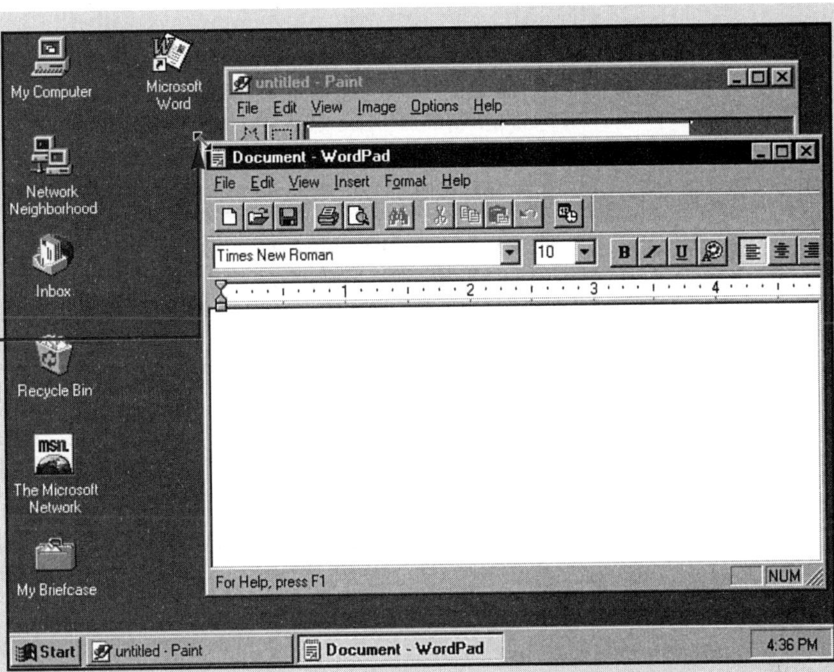

5 Drag the mouse pointer up and to the left to expand the window; then release the mouse button.

When you drag a window corner, you can change the size of two sides at the same time. In this case, both the top and left sides of the window move together. Dragging the diagonal two-headed arrow *into* the window shrinks the window.

6 Move the mouse pointer to the WordPad window title bar.

You can move a window around on the desktop by clicking and dragging its title bar.

7 Click and drag the title bar to move the window to the upper-left corner of the desktop.

This action moves the WordPad window to the upper-left corner of the desktop. When you move a window, an outline of the entire window appears so you can see where the window will be positioned when you release the mouse button.

8 Release the mouse button.

Releasing the mouse button "drops" the window in the new location.

Although these methods give you more flexibility, the taskbar menu has three commands that will arrange your application windows for you. Next, you learn how to use these commands to arrange your application windows.

INSIDE Stuff

You can size and move windows with the arrow keys as well. Simply click the Control-menu box, then choose **M**ove or **S**ize. Press the left, right, up, and down arrow keys to move and size the windows on-screen. An outline appears as a guide so you can see what the window looks like. Press Enter when you are done.

You can use the drag-and-drop technique to move icons around on the desktop. You might want to arrange the icons you frequently use in easy-to-reach places. Should you encounter problems with this, make sure you turn off Auto Arrange. Right-click the desktop, choose Arrange **I**cons, then **A**uto Arrange.

Note that you cannot resize some windows. If you don't see the two-headed arrow, click the Control-menu box and see if the Size command appears on the Control menu. If it does, try using the arrow keys to size the window. If it doesn't appear, that window cannot be resized.

To Arrange Windows Automatically

1 Point to a blank space on the taskbar.

Make sure you point to a blank space and not a button that represents a program. Also make sure the standard mouse pointer is visible—not the black double-headed sizing arrow you get if you point to the taskbar border.

2 Click the right mouse button.

Clicking the right mouse button opens the taskbar Context menu (see Figure 2.10). If you point to the clock, your Context menu also has an option for adjusting the date and time on it.

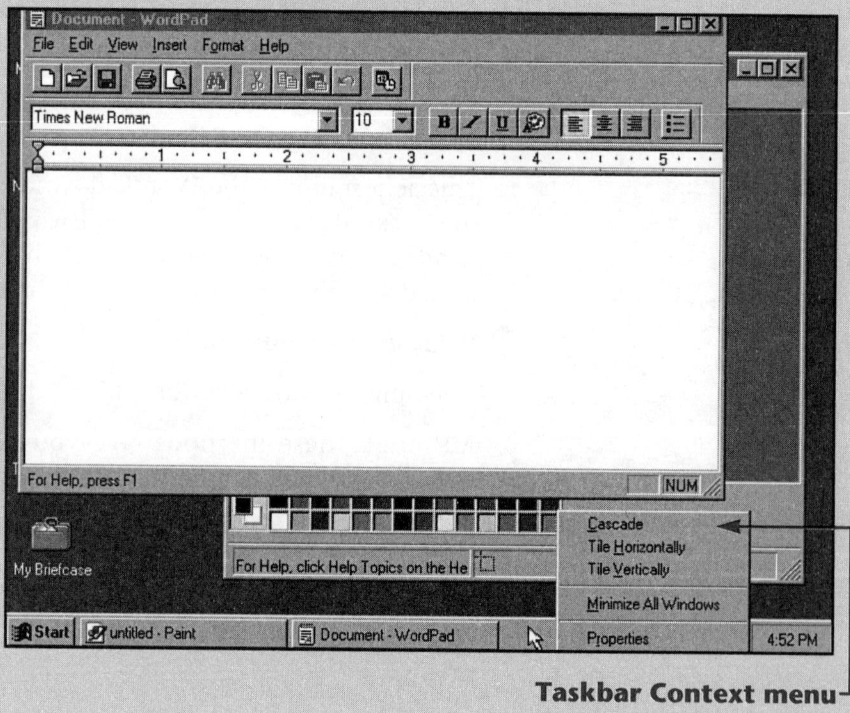

Figure 2.10
The taskbar Context menu has the **C**ascade and **T**ile commands.

If you have problems...

If you click the left mouse button, nothing happens. Try again with the right mouse button.

❸ Choose Cascade.

The **C**ascade command displays all open application windows, with the title bars cascading downward (see Figure 2.11). One application window is on top; the others are hidden behind. You can identify each window by its title bar. To switch back and forth between the application windows, just click anywhere in the window (in the title bar, document window, or scroll bar).

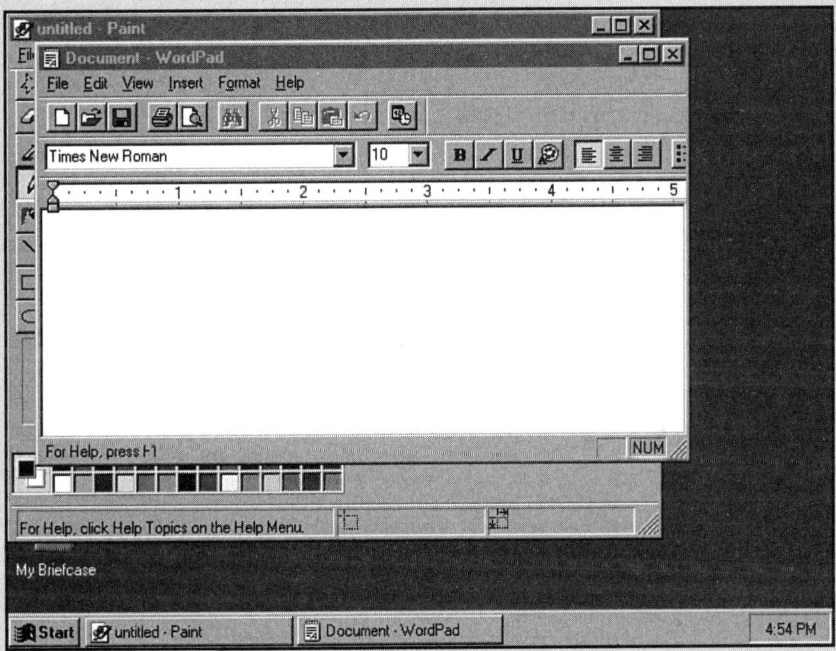

Figure 2.11
With cascaded application windows, you can easily locate the window you need.

❹ Right-click a blank space on the taskbar.

❺ Choose Tile Horizontally.

Horizontally tiling application windows divides the desktop evenly among the open programs and then sizes the windows to fit one above the other (see Figure 2.12). Because two applications are open, each application window takes up half of the space on the desktop.

❻ Right-click a blank space on the taskbar.

continues

To Arrange Windows Automatically (continued)

7 Choose Tile Vertically.

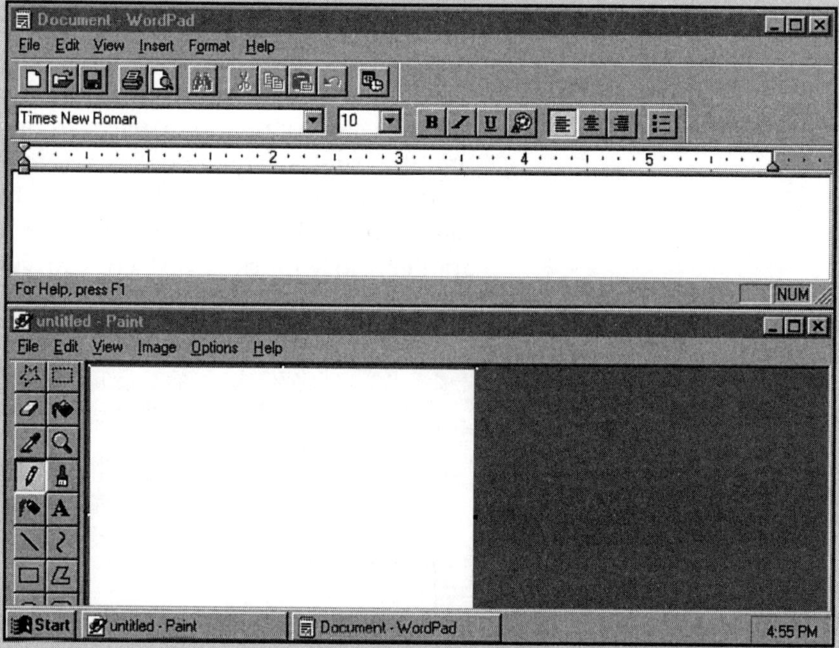

Figure 2.12
The WordPad and Paint windows are tiled horizontally, one above the other.

Vertically tiling application windows divides the desktop evenly among the open programs and then sizes the windows to fit side by side on the desktop (see Figure 2.13). Arranging windows side by side makes it easy to see information in several programs at once. Because you can cut and copy information between programs in Windows, the Tile Vertically option is popular. Leave the windows arranged as they are now for the next lesson.

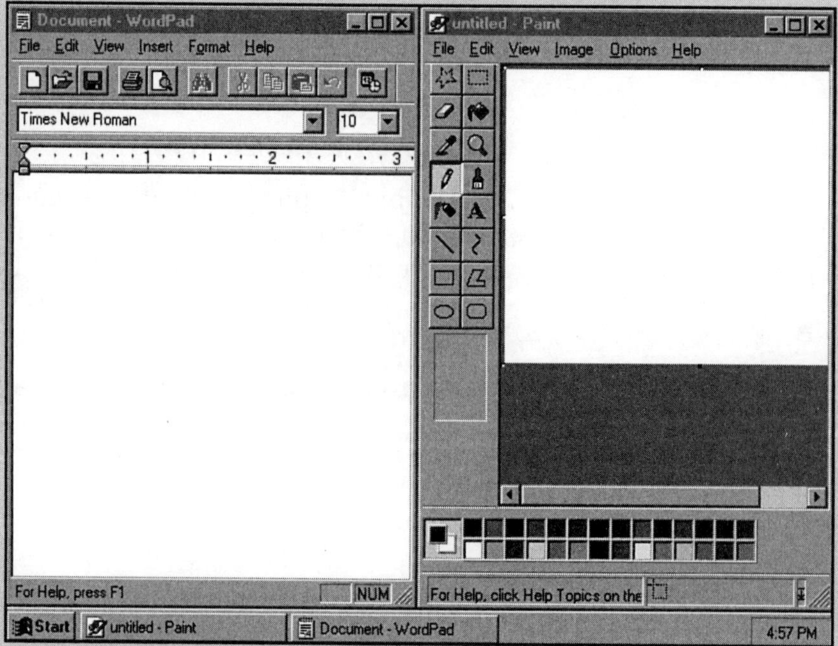

Figure 2.13
The WordPad and Paint windows are tiled vertically, side by side.

INSIDE Stuff

If you decide you don't like the way your windows are arranged after you choose the Cascade or Tile commands, you can choose one of the Undo commands on the taskbar Context menu. The **U**ndo Tile or **U**ndo Cascade commands switch the windows back to the state (size and position on the desktop) they were in when you selected the Tile or Cascade command. The Undo commands only appear on the taskbar Context menu *after* you choose a Cascade or Tile command.

Lesson 4: Maximizing, Minimizing, and Restoring a Window

Minimize
To reduce a window to a button.

When you *minimize* an application window, it shrinks the window to a button on the taskbar. Even though you can't see the window anymore, the application stays loaded in the computer's memory. Minimizing an application instead of closing it means you don't have to reload the program to use it.

Minimizing windows is like putting documents you want to use later in a folder off to the side of your desk. When you need the documents, you open the folder instead of searching through your file cabinet again.

Maximize
To increase the size of a window so it fills the entire screen.

You can also *maximize* a window so it fills the entire screen. This feature is useful if you want to see the largest area of a document (spreadsheet, letter, or drawing, for example). You might have noticed in the earlier lessons that the Paint and WordPad windows do not take up the entire screen. You can maximize both of these windows if you want more room to work in. However, you cannot maximize the Calculator window—it can only be minimized. Although there are exceptions to the rule, you will find that most of the windows you work in can be either maximized or minimized.

Practice maximizing and minimizing the WordPad window now.

To Maximize, Minimize, and Restore a Window

1. **Click the WordPad title bar.**

   Clicking the WordPad title bar selects the WordPad window. You can now work with this window.

2. **Click the Maximize button in the WordPad window.**

   The Maximize button is the middle button on the right side of the title bar. Clicking the Maximize button expands the WordPad window to full-screen size, completely covering the desktop (see Figure 2.14). The Maximize button turns into a Restore button, which has two stacked windows on it. Notice that maximizing a window still leaves room for the taskbar.

continues

To Maximize, Minimize, and Restore a Window (continued)

Figure 2.14
The WordPad window is now maximized.

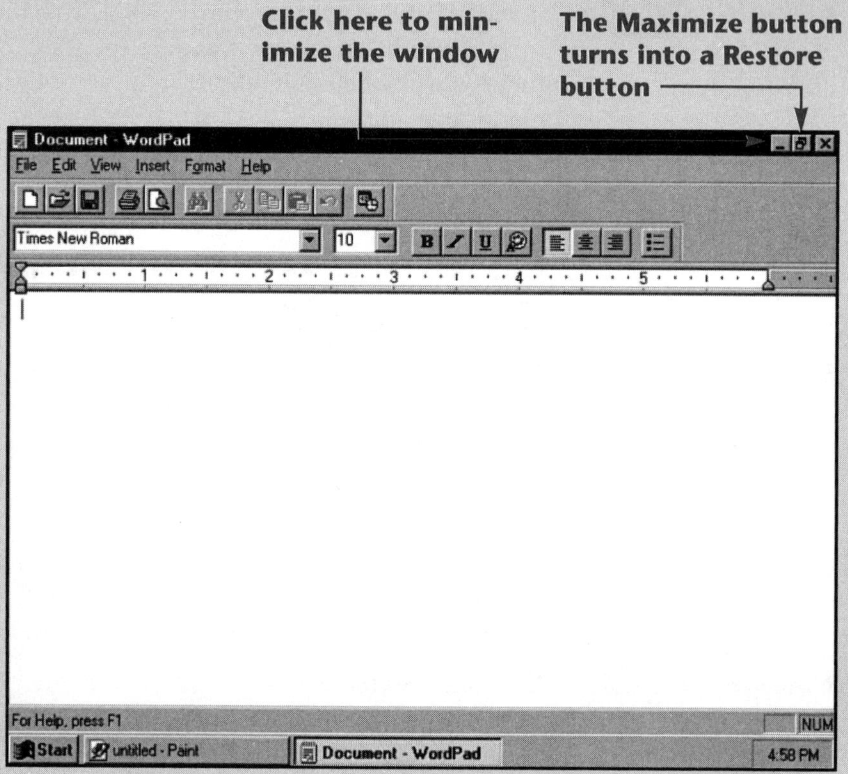

3 Click the Restore button in the WordPad window.

The window is now in a Restore state—the state it was in before you maximized it (see Figure 2.15). Restoring full-screen programs down into windows lets you see (and work with) more than one program at a time.

By clicking the Minimize or Maximize button, you can minimize or maximize a window when it's in the Restore state.

4 Click the Minimize button in the WordPad window.

Clicking the Minimize button shrinks the WordPad window to a WordPad button on the taskbar (see Figure 2.16). Windows uses a special effect to illustrate graphically the shrinking or expanding when a window is minimized or maximized.

Even though you can no longer see the WordPad window, the program is still running. You should always click the taskbar button to reopen an application window—don't start a second copy of the program!

Figure 2.15
The WordPad window is in a Restore state.

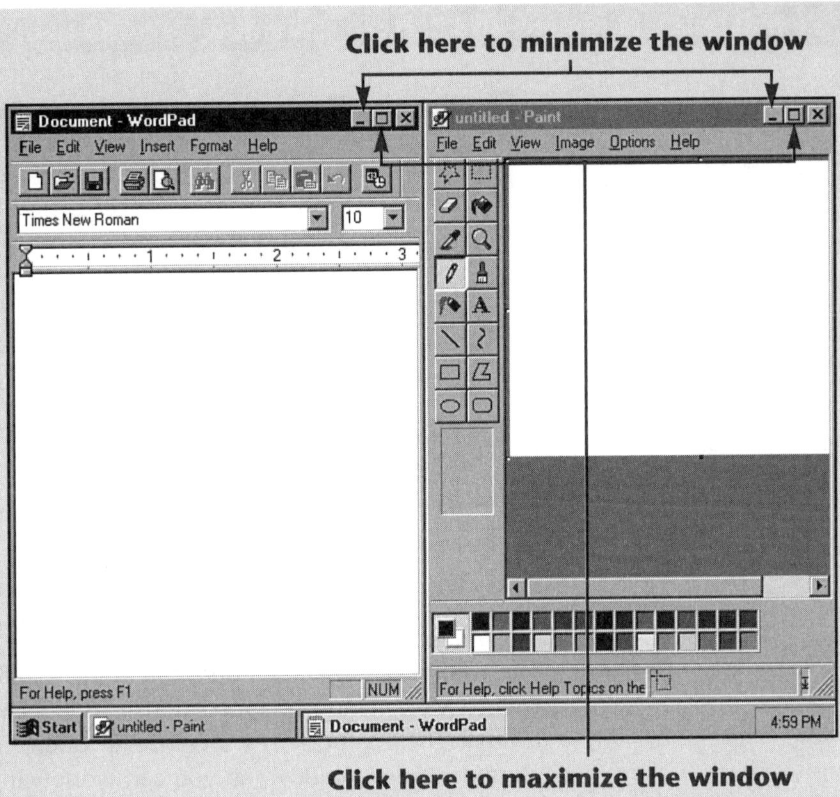

Figure 2.16
The WordPad window is minimized to a button on the taskbar.

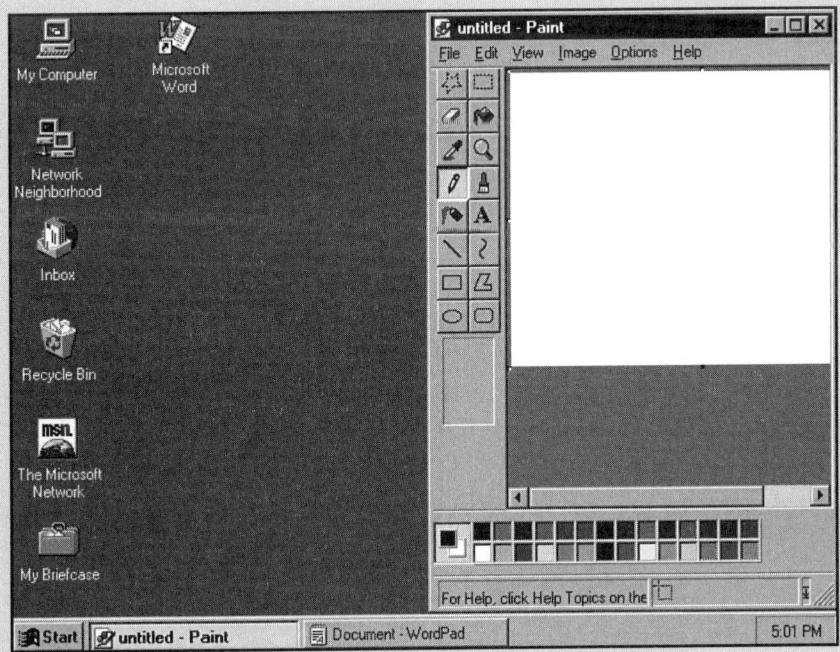

5 Click the WordPad button on the taskbar.

Clicking the WordPad button opens the WordPad window. Notice that the window automatically returns to the state it was in when you minimized it.

continues

To Maximize, Minimize, and Restore a Window (continued)

6. **Click the Maximize button in the Paint window.**

   The Paint window expands to fill the screen, so it is maximized. Now restore it.

7. **Click the Restore button in the Paint window.**

   The Paint window returns to its preceding size and position.

8. **Resize and move the WordPad and Paint windows back to their original positions before you used the Tile commands.**

   This step is optional; complete it only if you want to practice the skills you learned in Lesson 3.

INSIDE Stuff

If you want to minimize all the open windows at once, right-click a blank space on the taskbar and choose **M**inimize All Windows.

The commands discussed here can apply also to documents you use in an application. Most Windows applications can work with more than one document at a time. These programs allow you to open, minimize, maximize, restore, and close *document* windows so you can work with multiple documents at the same time. Minimizing a document window shrinks the document to an icon on the application workspace.

Lesson 5: Closing an Application Window

When you close an application window, you exit the application. If you made changes you haven't saved yet, the program prompts you to save those changes. There is a very important difference between closing an application window and minimizing an application window. When you minimize an application window, the application is still running, so you can switch back to it at any time. When you close an application window, you exit the application; if you want to go back to the application, you must start it again. Close the Paint and WordPad application windows now.

To Close an Application Window

1. **Click the Close button in the WordPad window.**

   Clicking the Close button closes the WordPad window, exiting the program (see Figure 2.17). Now close the Paint program.

Close button

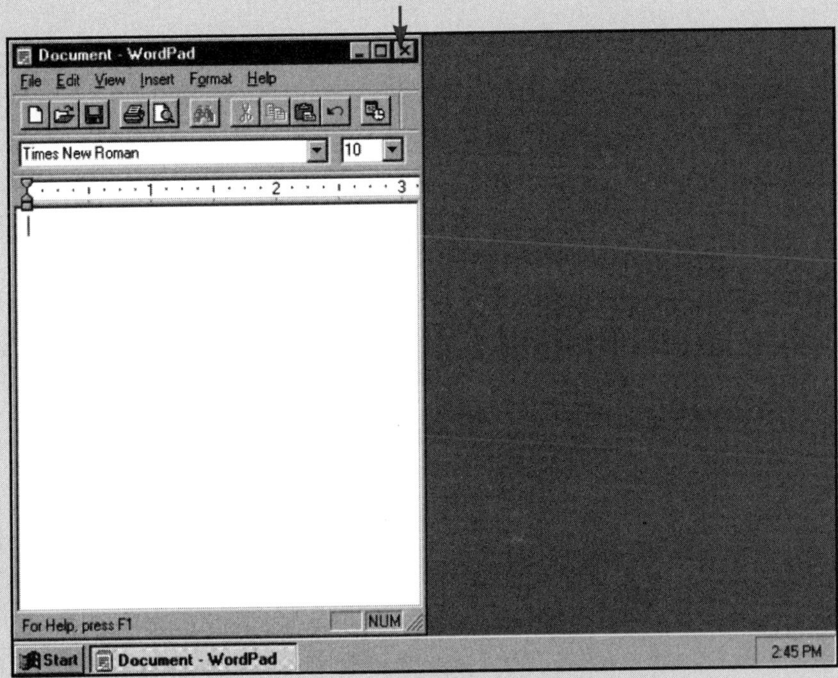

Figure 2.17
The Close button closes the window, exiting the program.

If you have problems...

If you have made any changes to the WordPad document (even inadvertently), Windows prompts you to save those changes. If this happens, answer **N**o—do not save the changes.

2 Click the Close button in the Paint window.

This closes the Paint window, exiting the program. The WordPad and Paint buttons should no longer appear on the taskbar.

If you have completed your session on the computer, shut down the Windows program before turning off the computer. Otherwise, continue with the "Applying Your Skills" section.

INSIDE Stuff

There are several other methods for closing an application window. You can double-click the application Control-menu box, or click the application Control-menu box and choose **C**lose. You can also press Alt+F4, or pull down the **F**ile menu and choose E**x**it.

Summary

To	Do This
Start an application	Click the Start button. Move the mouse pointer up to highlight **P**rograms. Move the mouse pointer to the right to move into the Programs menu. Highlight the program folder that contains the program, then click the icon.
Switch between application windows	Click the application button on the taskbar, or click anywhere inside the application window, or press Alt+Esc until the window you want is at the top of the stack, or press Alt+Tab until the blue box surrounds the icon that represents the program you want to work with.
Move a window	Click and drag the title bar. Release the mouse button to place the window in the new location.
Size a window	Point to a window border. When the two-headed arrow appears, click and drag the border. Release the mouse button to resize the window.
Tile multiple program windows	Right-click the taskbar, then choose Tile **H**orizontally or Tile **V**ertically.
Cascade multiple program windows	Right-click the taskbar, then choose **C**ascade.
Undo a tile or cascade	Right-click the taskbar, then choose **U**ndo Cascade or **U**ndo Tile.
Maximize a window	Click the Maximize button (it looks like a box with a thick line on the top).
Minimize a window	Click the Minimize button (it looks like a dash).
Restore a window	Click the Restore button (it looks like two cascading windows).
Close a window	Click the Close button (it looks like an X).

Applying Your Skills

These "On Your Own" exercises enable you to practice the skills you have learned in this project. Take a few minutes to work through these exercises now.

On Your Own

Becoming Familiar with the Taskbar Menu

For each option in the left column, define its purpose in the right column.

Taskbar Menu Option	Definition
Minimize All Windows	
Tile Vertically	
CascadeTile Horizontally	

Opening Windows 95 Applications

In this exercise, you open three applications, tile them, cascade them, switch between them, and close them.

1. Click the Start button and choose Programs, Accessories, Paint.
2. Using the same steps, open Notepad from the Accessories folder.
3. Using the same steps, open WordPad from the Accessories folder.
4. Right-click the taskbar to open the taskbar menu. Tile the three application windows horizontally. Undo the tile arrangement.
5. Cascade the application windows. Undo the cascade arrangement.
6. Switch among the three applications windows by using the taskbar buttons, using the shortcut keys, or clicking in the windows.
7. Close all three applications.

Working with Program Windows

In this exercise, you practice moving, resizing, minimizing, and maximizing a program window.

1. Click the Start button and choose Programs, Accessories, Games, Solitaire. Move the Solitaire window around on the desktop by pointing to the title bar and dragging the window to new locations. Then place the window in the center of the screen.
2. Move the mouse pointer across the right border of the window until it changes from a white selection arrow to a black, double-sided resizing arrow. Resize the window so that only three rows of cards are showing. Then resize the window so that it is back to its original size (you should see seven rows of cards).

3. Move the mouse pointer across the lower-right corner until a diagonal resizing arrow is displayed. Resize the window to approximately half its original size by dragging two sides at once. Then drag the corner back to its original location.
4. Maximize the Solitaire window so it takes up the entire screen.
5. Restore the window by clicking the Restore button.
6. Minimize Solitaire. Notice that a button for the program appears on the taskbar, indicating that the program is still running in memory.
7. Click the taskbar button for Solitaire. The program is displayed again in a desktop window.
8. Close the Solitaire program by clicking the Close button. Note that there is no longer a taskbar button shown for the program.

Switching between Program Windows

1. Open Solitaire and then Minesweeper by using the Start, **P**rograms, Accessories, Games sequence. Click in the Solitaire window, making it the active window. Notice that the title bar is blue and the taskbar button for Solitaire is indented.
2. Click the taskbar button for Minesweeper. When it is selected, it becomes the active window and moves to the top of the stack, on top of the Solitaire window.
3. Open the taskbar's Context menu and choose **M**inimize All Windows. Both programs are minimized into buttons on the taskbar.
4. Click the button for Minesweeper. The program is selected as the active program and restored to its previous size and location.
5. Click the button for Solitaire. This switches the "attention" of the computer to that program and makes Solitaire the active program as it restores it.
6. Press Alt+Tab a number of times to switch between the actively running programs.
7. Minimize both programs.
8. Click the Solitaire button to restore it.
9. Close Solitaire by clicking the Close button.
10. Close Minesweeper by right-clicking the button to open the Context menu and then choosing **C**lose. Note that the buttons for Minesweeper and Solitaire are no longer displayed on the taskbar.

Project 3

Working with My Computer

Objectives

In this project, you learn how to

- ➤ Work with My Computer
- ➤ Arrange Folder Windows
- ➤ Display File Information
- ➤ Select Files and Folders
- ➤ Create New Folders

Why Would I Do This?

One of the most important skills you can learn is how to manage your files. After all, what good is a well-thought-out, carefully prepared document (or spreadsheet) if you can't find it later? My Computer is a powerful yet easy-to-use feature that helps you organize and manage files.

Lesson 1: Working with My Computer

When you work on a file in an application, such as Microsoft Word, you are working in the computer's *memory* (or *RAM*), which is a temporary storage location. If you lose power, the memory is erased, so unless you have saved your work to a *floppy disk* or *hard disk drive*, you lose your work. Floppy disks and hard disks are considered to be permanent storage because they keep your saved work even after you turn off the computer.

When you save a file, you have to give the file a unique name. Windows 95 recognizes two different types of file names. The first type of file name follows the traditional DOS rules of an eight-character name followed by a period and an optional three-character extension. Most of the programs available today use the DOS file-name rules. Applications designed for earlier releases of Windows assign their own extensions. For example, Microsoft Word uses DOC, Excel uses XLS, and PowerPoint uses PPT. However, most people find these file names restrictive—it's hard to come up with a meaningful name with just 11 characters.

One of the most popular enhancements in Windows 95 is the capability of naming a file with up to 255 characters. For example, instead of using TAYLOR.PRP, you can use a file name of Proposal for Taylor Engineering - 611 Peacock Project. Only Windows 95 applications and those written for Windows 95 can see these long file names. Older versions of Windows programs and DOS programs see a traditional file name for those files. (Windows 95 assigns the shorter, DOS file name automatically when you save a file with a long file name).

Over time, you might create hundreds of files that need to be organized so you can find them when you need them again. To make the job of organizing your files easier, you can organize your hard disk into folders and subfolders. Here is an analogy: think of your hard disk as a filing cabinet and of the folders as drawers in the filing cabinet. In a filing cabinet, each drawer can hold a different category of documents. In a hard disk, each folder can hold a different category of files that can be either applications or documents. In a filing cabinet drawer, you can add hanging file folders to divide the drawer further. In the same way, you can subdivide a folder on your hard disk by creating subfolders that can also hold files. Most people use the terms *folder* and *subfolder* interchangeably.

Take a look at My Computer now.

To Work with My Computer

1 Double-click the My Computer icon.

Double-clicking this icon opens a window for the My Computer application (see Figure 3.1). My Computer has an icon for each drive on your system; icons for the Control Panel and Printers; and, in this case, an icon for Dial-Up Networking. The idea behind My Computer is to give you quick access to all the resources on your system.

Figure 3.1
My Computer contains icons for the drives on your system.

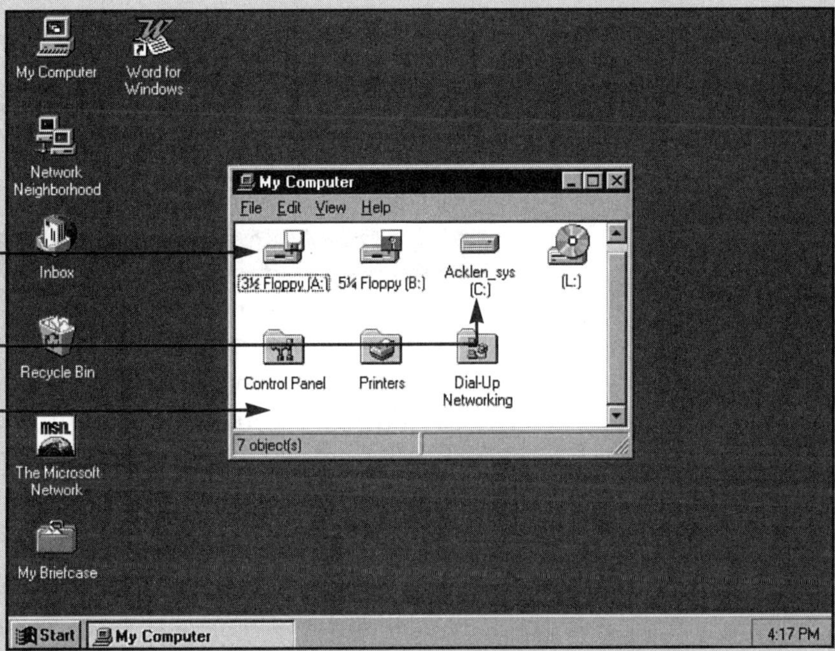

If you have problems...

If your system has additional equipment installed, or if you are on a network, your My Computer window will look different. For example, if you have a CD-ROM drive available, an icon for a CD drive would also appear. If you don't have a 5 1/4-inch drive, there will be no icon for that drive.

---

2 Double-click the hard drive icon.

Double-clicking a drive icon opens a window with the folders and files found on that drive (see Figure 3.2). The folders and files are shown alphabetically from left to right. Folders are listed first, followed by the files. The name of the drive (or folder) in the window appears in the title bar.

continues

To Work with my Computer (continued)

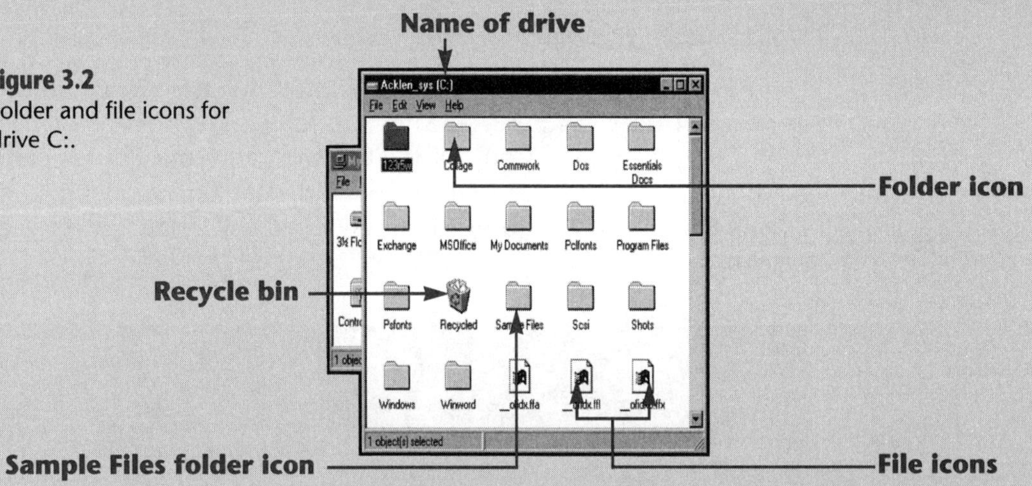

Figure 3.2
Folder and file icons for drive C:.

If you have problems...

The hard drive in a computer is usually called drive C:. Depending on how your system has been set up, you might need to look for a different drive icon, like drive D: or E:. My Computer shows you the drives that are available on the computer. If you need to access a network drive, use the Network Neighborhood application. Ask your instructor for assistance in locating the correct drive.

The icons in your window might look different if the **V**iew settings have been changed. Don't worry about it—you'll have a chance to change the settings later in this lesson.

3 Double-click the Sample Files folder icon.

Double-clicking a folder icon opens a folder window with the subfolders and files in that folder. Each time you open a folder window, a button for that window appears on the taskbar (see Figure 3.3).

Figure 3.3
The Sample files folder.

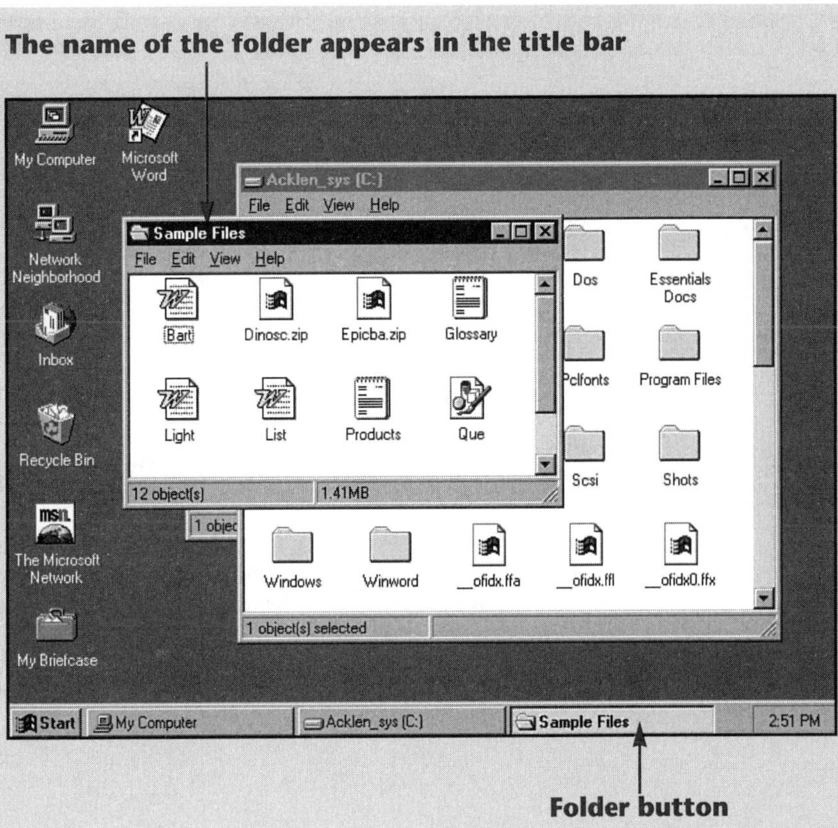

If you have problems...

If you have only one window on the desktop and one folder button on the taskbar (you should have three), your **V**iew settings have been changed. Choose **V**iew and then choose **O**ptions. Click the Browse folders using a **s**eparate window for each folder option button and then click OK. With this setting on, Windows will open a separate window for each folder.

4 Click the down scroll arrow on the vertical scroll bar.

Scroll down through the window to see the rest of the folders and files. Windows uses many types of file icons to illustrate the type of file (see Table 3.1 for descriptions of commonly used icons). The name of the folder or file is shown below the icon (see Figure 3.4).

continues

To Work with My Computer (continued)

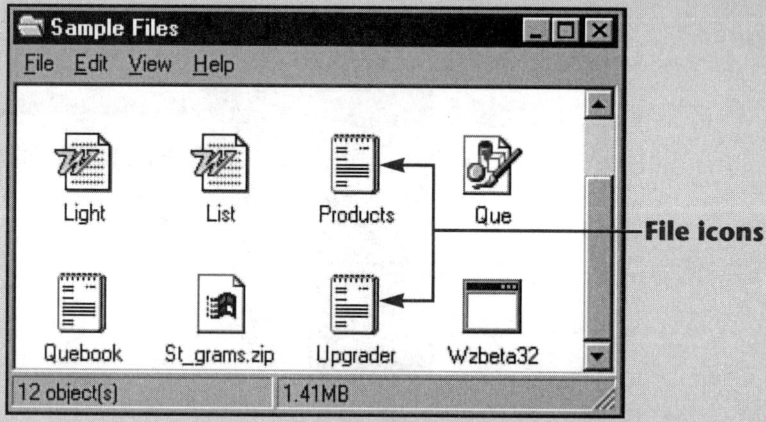

Figure 3.4
Windows uses a variety of file icons to illustrate file types.

Table 3.1 Commonly Used File Icons

File Icon	Description
	Bitmap image
	Help file
	System file
	Configuration settings file
	Program group file
	Wave sound file
	Text document file
	Miscellaneous file

You now have a series of folder windows open on the desktop. Leave the desktop in this state for the next lesson, where you learn how to arrange folder windows.

Jargon Watch

Memory (or **RAM**) is a computer's temporary storage area, as distinguished from permanent storage areas, such as floppy and hard disk drives. A **floppy disk** is a removable storage medium that uses a thin flexible disk enclosed in a plastic envelope or case. A **hard disk drive** is a nonremovable storage medium, composed of a disk or several disks stacked one on top of each other and sealed inside a metal case that is installed inside your computer.

A **folder** is an area on a disk (hard or floppy) that can contain files and other folders grouped together by type or category. A **subfolder** is a folder within another folder. **Folder windows** display folders and files within a folder.

Folder icons represent folders in My Computer. **Drive icons** represent drives on your computer. You might see drive icons for floppy drives, hard drives, tape drives, and CD-ROM drives.

In Figure 3.2, a Recycled icon is shown. This icon represents the Recycle Bin, an area where Windows keeps deleted files. You can retrieve from the Recycle Bin any files you accidentally delete.

Windows 95 has another file-management tool, called The Explorer. The Explorer closely resembles the Windows 3.x File Manager.

Lesson 2: Arranging Folder Windows

As in most Windows applications, you can work with more than one window at a time in My Computer. You can open multiple windows, each showing the contents of a different drive or folder. When you need to move and copy files between folders, make backup copies to a floppy disk, or delete files, folder windows provide easy access to your files.

You can arrange folder windows with the same methods you used to arrange application windows in Project 2. As you have seen, you can arrange windows manually, by sizing and moving them, or you can position them automatically with the Cascade and Tile commands. Try the Cascade and Tile commands on the folder windows, then arrange the Windows folder window to get ready for Lesson 3.

To Arrange Folder Windows

1 Right-click a blank space on the taskbar.

Right-clicking the taskbar opens the taskbar Context menu. As you can see, you use the same commands you used in Project 2 to arrange application windows to arrange folder windows. This time around, use the Undo commands to undo the arrangement.

2 Choose Cascade.

The **C**ascade command arranges one folder window on top of another, with the title bars cascading downward (see Figure 3.5). The Sample files folder window is on top, and the others are hidden underneath.

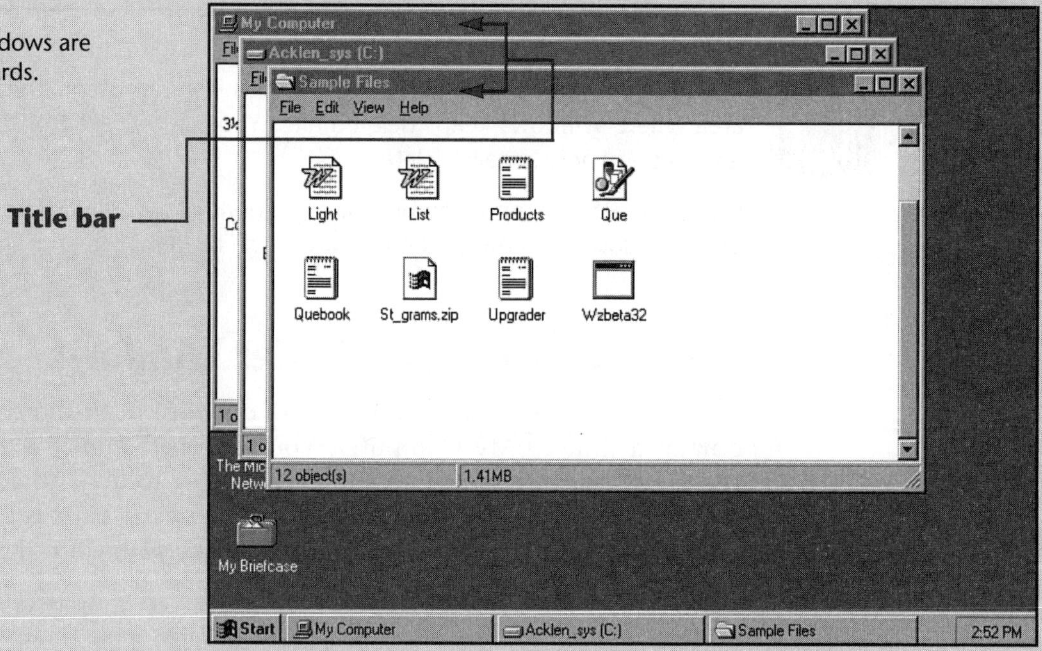

Figure 3.5
Cascaded windows are stacked like cards.

3 Right-click the taskbar and choose Undo Cascade.

The **U**ndo Cascade command switches back to the arrangement of windows before you chose the **C**ascade command. If you decide you don't like the cascade arrangement, this is the fastest way to put things back the way they were.

4 Right-click the taskbar and choose Tile Horizontally.

The My Computer and folder windows are now tiled horizontally on the desktop (see Figure 3.6). This is a popular arrangement for moving and copying files between folders. When you finish, you can put the folder windows back the way they were with the Undo Tile command.

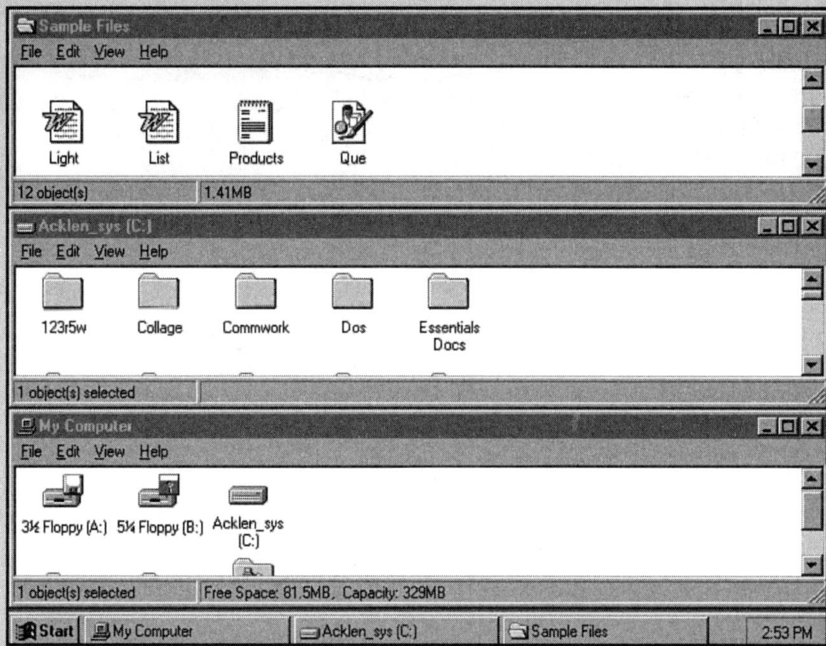

Figure 3.6
The windows are tiled horizontally.

5 Right-click the taskbar and choose Undo Tile.

Like the **U**ndo Cascade command, the **U**ndo Tile command switches the windows back to their original positions. Now, arrange the folder windows to get ready for the next lesson.

6 Click Sample Files on the taskbar.

Clicking the Sample Files button moves the Sample files folder window to the top of the stack. The files in the Sample Files folder are used as sample files in the next lesson.

7 Click the Maximize button on the Sample Files folder window title bar.

Clicking the Maximize button expands the folder window to full size (see Figure 3.7). Maximizing a folder window creates more room, so you can see more folders and files.

continues

To Arrange Folder Windows (continued)

Figure 3.7
The Sample Files folder window is maximized on the desktop.

Leave the desktop in its current state for the next lesson, where you learn how to display additional file information.

INSIDE Stuff

To switch back and forth between folder windows, just click the folder button on the taskbar to switch to that window.

Lesson 3: Displaying File Information

Figure 3.7 shows icons representing folders and files in the Windows folder in a large size for easy identification. You can use smaller icons instead, enabling you to see more files in the window. You can display the file size, file type, and the revision date and time.

Folders and files are usually sorted by name, but you can sort them by date, size, and type if you prefer. For example, you might want to find a file you created on a particular date, or you might want to find the largest files so you can take them off your system to make room on the disk. Try displaying different kinds of file information now.

To Display File Information

1 Choose View from the Sample Files folder menu bar.

The **V**iew menu appears, as shown in Figure 3.8. In the first section of the menu, the check mark next to the Status **B**ar option tells you that the status bar is selected (it is displayed). The **T**oolbar option doesn't have a check mark because this option isn't currently selected.

The next section in the **V**iew menu has four options—Lar**g**e Icons is currently selected. In this group, you can select only one option at a time, so a bullet is used to indicate the current setting.

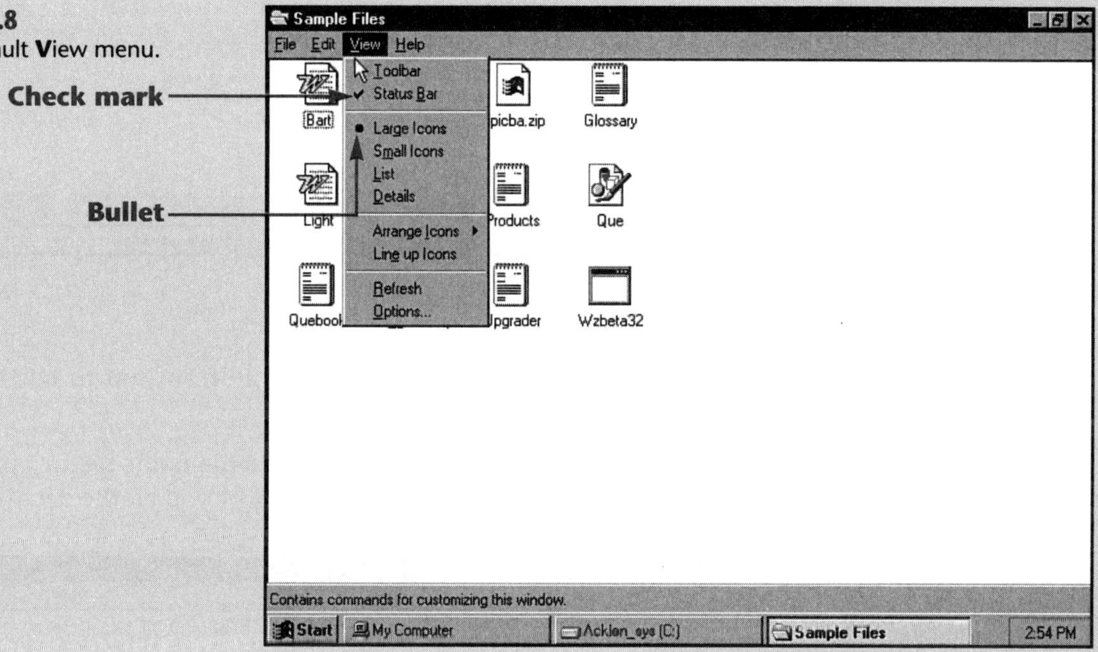

Figure 3.8
The default **V**iew menu.

If you have problems...

If your settings are different from these, they have been changed since the program was installed. Choose Status **B**ar and Lar**g**e Icons to reset the settings to the defaults.

2 Choose Small Icons.

This option uses smaller icons in the window, enabling you to see more files at one time (see Figure 3.9). The files are sorted alphabetically (folders first and then files), but they are ordered in columns from left to right. It might be hard to find a file alphabetically with this setting.

continues

To Display File Information (continued)

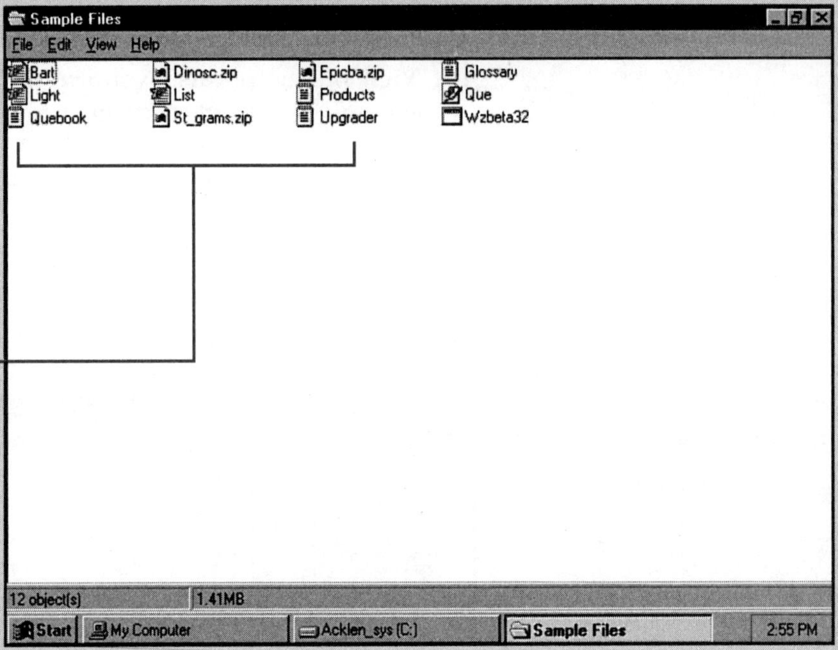

Figure 3.9
The Sample Files folder with small icons.

Files are ordered from left to right

❸ **Choose View, List.**

The folders are now listed alphabetically from top to bottom (see Figure 3.10).

Up to this point, you have seen only the file name next to the icon. Next, you change the **V**iew setting to show you all the details.

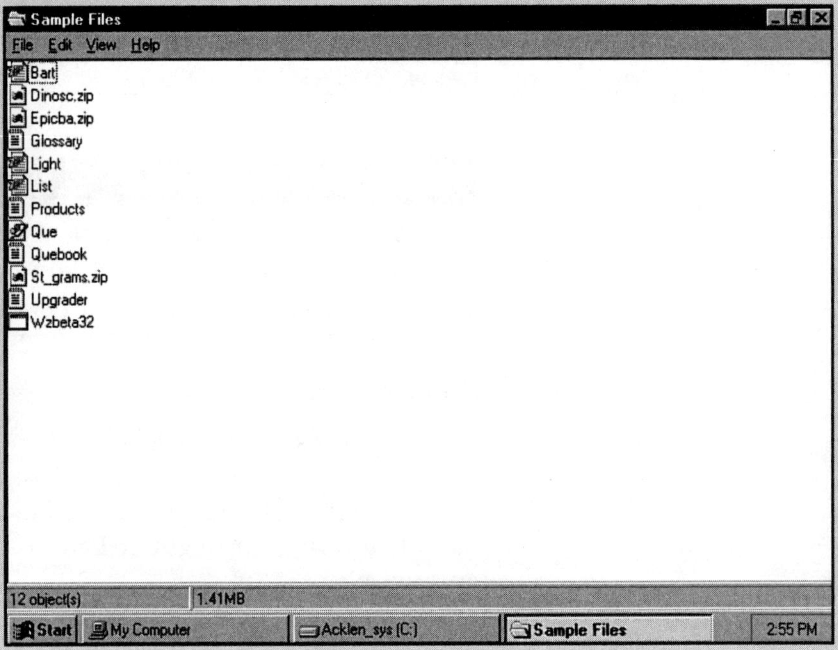

Figure 3.10
The Sample Files folder with the **L**ist option chosen.

4 Choose View, Details.

Now you can see the following information for the folders at the top of the list: name, type, and modification date and time (see Figure 3.11).

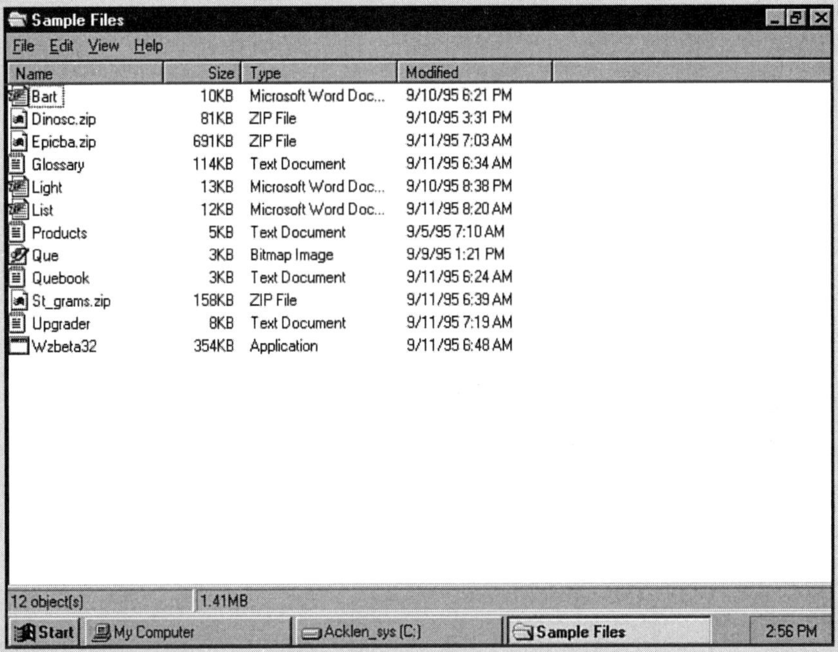

Figure 3.11
The contents of the Sample Files folder with additional details shown.

5 Click the down scroll arrow until you can see the file icons.

This step isn't really necessary, but moving down into the file icons helps illustrate the following features more clearly. Notice that the Size column shows a size for each file (but not the folders).

Currently, the files are arranged by their names. Try the other options now.

6 Choose View, Arrange Icons.

Choosing Arrange **I**cons opens a submenu with four different options to choose from.

7 Choose By Type.

The By **T**ype command arranges the icons by type. In Figure 3.12, for example, the application files are grouped together.

continues

To Display File Information (continued)

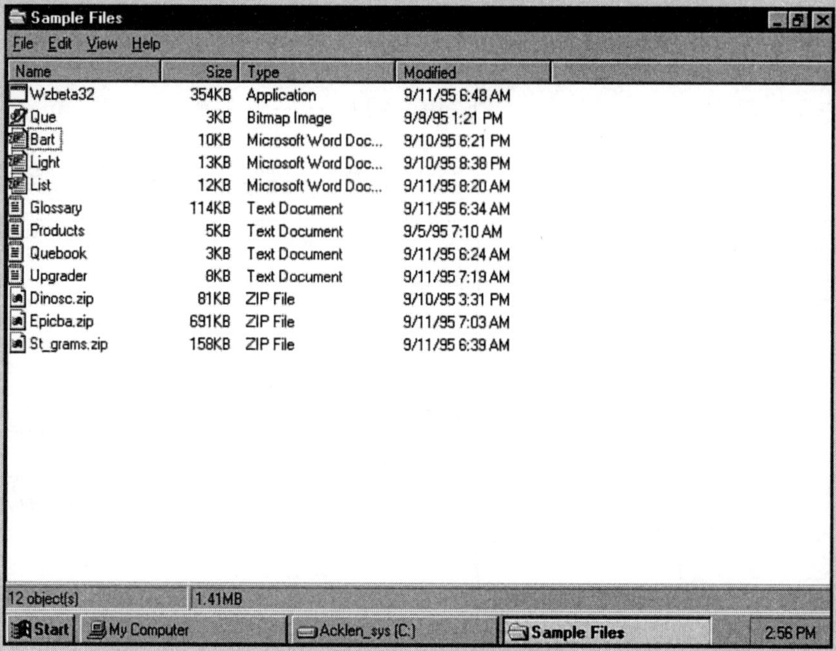

Figure 3.12
The icons in the Sample Files folder, grouped together by type.

8 Choose View, Arrange Icons, and then By Date.

The By **D**ate command sorts files by last date saved, from newest to oldest (see Figure 3.13). Arranging files by date makes it easy to locate the files you revised in a given time period.

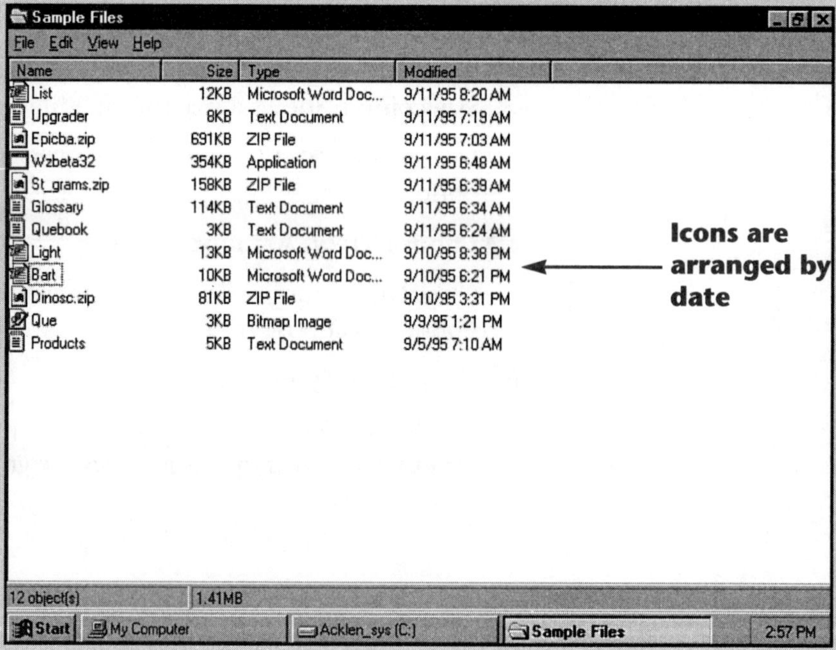

Figure 3.13
The icons are now sorted by date.

9 Choose View, Arrange Icons, and then By Name.

The list should now be sorted alphabetically by the file name, which is the default setting.

10 Choose View, List.

The window should now contain only the icons and the icon names. Leave the Windows folder window open and in this state for the next lesson.

INSIDE Stuff

You also can choose **V**iew, Arrange **I**cons, By Si**z**e to arrange the files by their size, from smallest to largest. Also, you don't have to choose **D**etails (to display the file date or size in the window) to arrange the icons by those attributes. For example, you don't have to see the file sizes to arrange the icons by size (it's just easier to see the results). Also, you can click the column heading to sort by that entry.

Lesson 4: Selecting Folders and Files

The primary rule of all Windows programs is *select, then do*. You must first find and select a folder or file before you can act on it (open, cut, copy, delete, or display properties). Project 4 covers actions you can take on folders and files.

Using the mouse, you can quickly select one or more folder or file icons. In this lesson, you select files. However, you can use the same techniques on folders. Try selecting files now.

To Select Folders and Files

1 Click the Glossary.txt file icon in the Sample Files folder window.

A single click on a file or folder selects it. When you select a file, a selection bar appears (see Figure 3.14). The status bar has indicators that tell you how many files are selected and how large (in *bytes*) the files are.

2 Click the Quebook.txt file.

When you select another file in the list, the first file is no longer selected. To select more than one file, you have to use a different technique.

continues

To Select Files and Folders (continued)

Figure 3.14
The selected icon name is highlighted.

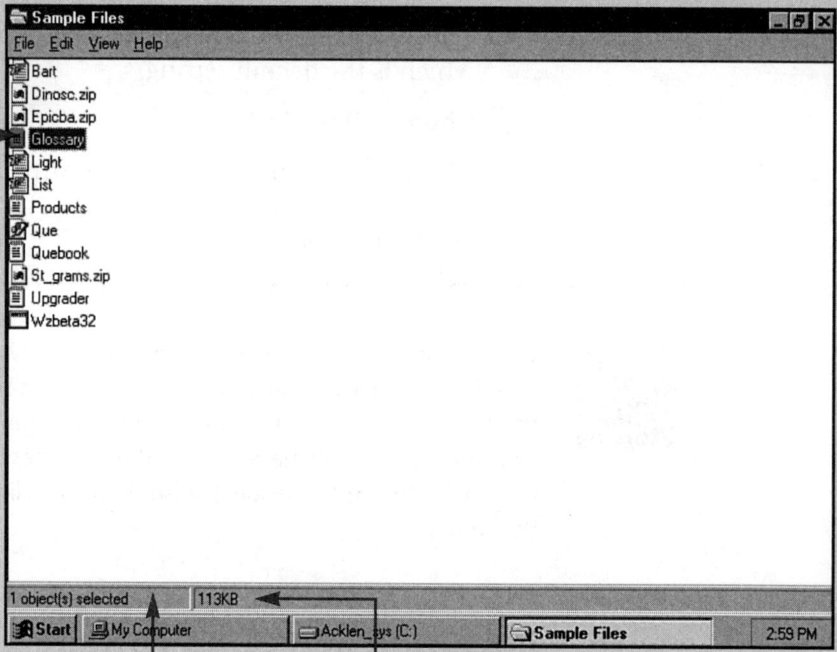

3 Hold down ⇧Shift and click the Products.txt file.

All the files between the first selected file and the file you selected with ⇧Shift are now selected (see Figure 3.15). This is the fastest way to select a series of adjacent files. The left side of the status bar tells you how many files you have selected and how many bytes they take up.

Figure 3.15
Adjacent files are selected.

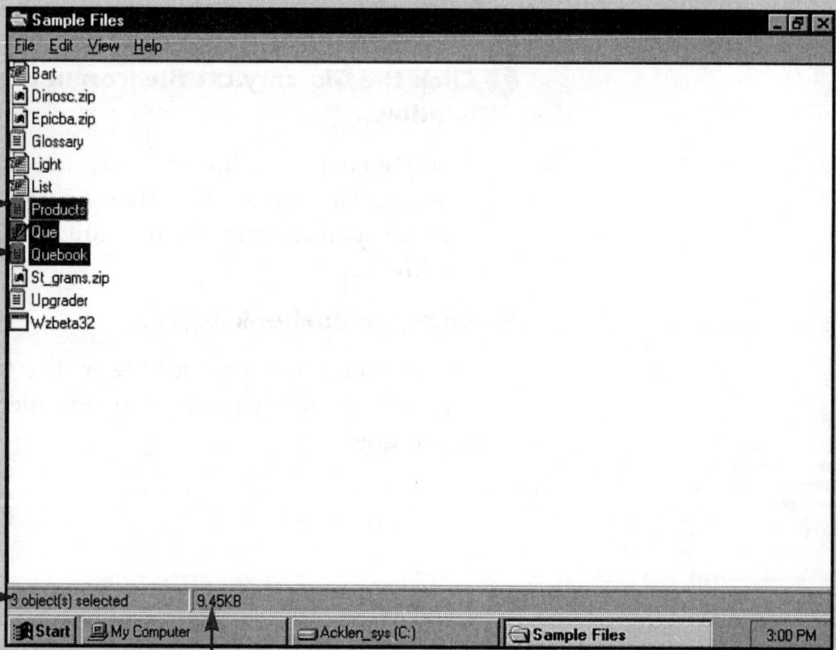

At some time, you will need to select several different files located in different areas of the folder window. These are called non-adjacent files because they are not grouped together in a continuous list. Try selecting non-adjacent files now.

4 Click the Que.bmp file.

The Que bitmap file is now selected and the adjacent files you selected in the preceding step are automatically deselected.

5 Press and hold down Ctrl; then click the Bart file, the Glossary file, and the Products file.

Four files are now selected. Your screen should look similar to Figure 3.16.

Figure 3.16
Selected non-adjacent files.

Selected non-adjacent files

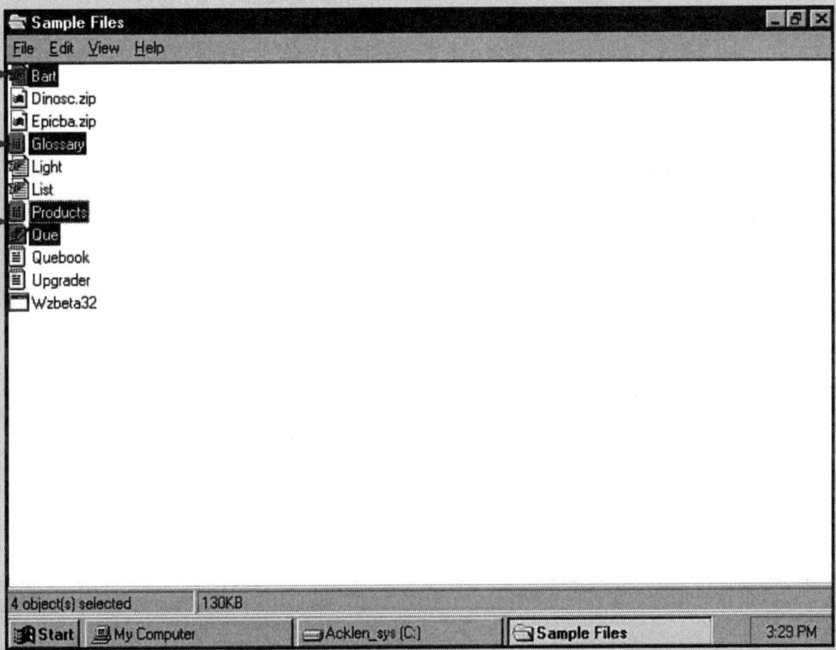

6 Press and hold down Ctrl while you click the Bart file.

The Bart file is deselected. You can deselect a particular file while retaining the other selections.

7 Scroll through the folder window until you can see the Wzbeta32 file.

You can select non-adjacent files in different parts of the contents list by scrolling until you can see the file.

8 Press and hold down Ctrl as you click the WZbeta32 file.

The left side of the status bar tells you that you have four files (objects) selected and tells you their combined size in K (kilobytes).

continues

To Select Files and Folders (continued)

9 Click the Close button.

Clicking the Close button closes the Windows folder window. The My Computer and hard drive windows should still be minimized as buttons on the taskbar. Leave the desktop in this state for the next lesson.

Jargon Watch

The total number of **bytes** shown on the status bar is the amount of space required to store the file(s) on disk. A byte is roughly equivalent to one character. The abbreviation for kilobyte is K, which is 1,024 bytes. The abbreviation for megabyte is M, which is 1,024,000 bytes.

Don't forget! You can also use the techniques discussed in this lesson to select folders.

Lesson 5: Creating New Folders

Creating new folders on a disk is like adding new drawers to a filing cabinet. This is a great way to reorganize or restructure your disk for new categories. After you create folders and subfolders, you can move or copy existing files into them.

Try creating new folders now.

To Create a New Folder

1 Insert a blank floppy disk into your floppy disk drive.

Using the same basic steps, you can create folder and subfolders on both floppy and hard drives. A floppy disk is used here and throughout the next project (when you learn how to copy, move, rename, and delete files).

2 Click the My Computer button on the taskbar.

Clicking this button moves the My Computer window to the top of the stack on the desktop.

3 Double-click the drive icon that represents the drive in which you inserted the disk.

Clicking the floppy drive icon opens a folder window on the desktop. If the floppy disk is blank, the window will be empty.

4 Choose File from the menu bar.

Choosing **F**ile opens the **F**ile menu (see Figure 3.17).

Figure 3.17
The folder window for the floppy disk is empty.

5 Choose New and then choose Folder.

A folder icon appears in the window (see Figure 3.18). The default folder name, `New Folder`, appears selected under the icon. When text is already selected, anything you type replaces the selection.

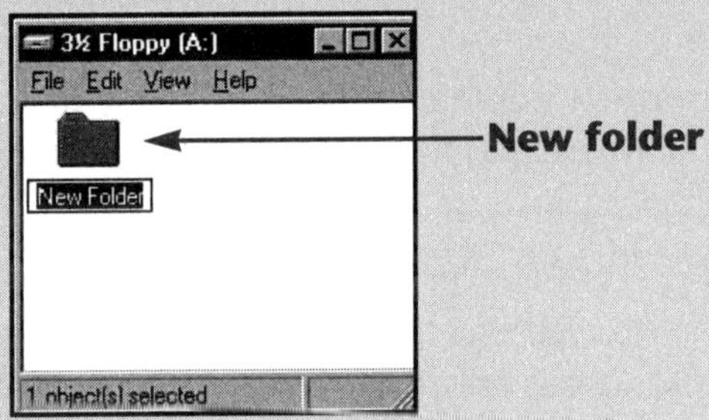

Figure 3.18
The new folder icon.

6 Type Loan Documents.

Folder names can be up to 255 characters long, just like file names. As you can see, the name can take up a lot of space under the icon, so you might want to keep the names short.

7 Press Enter.

You have now added a folder called Loan Documents on the floppy disk (see Figure 3.19). Now try adding a subfolder in this folder.

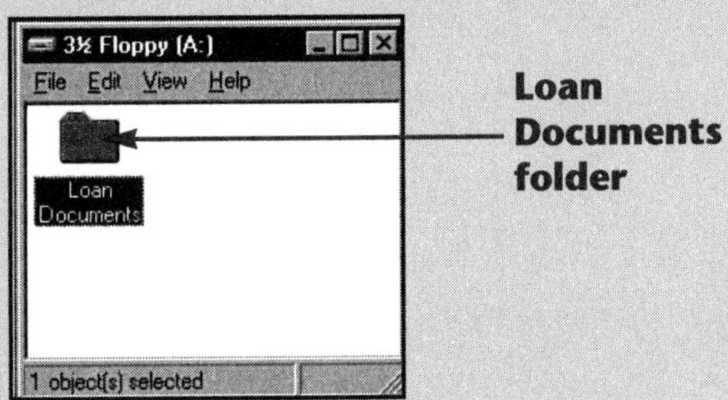

Figure 3.19
The new folder on the floppy disk.

continues

To Create a New Folder (continued)

8. **Double-click the Loan Documents folder icon.**

   This opens a folder window for the Loan Documents folder. This is where you want to create the subfolder.

9. **Choose File, New, Folder.**

   A new folder icon appears in the window.

10. **Type Car Loans.**

    You have just added the Car Loans subfolder to the Loan Documents folder. Leave these folders on the floppy disk for use in Project 4.

11. **Close all the open folder windows and My Computer.**

    If you have completed your session on the computer, remove the floppy disk, then shut down the Windows program before turning off the computer. Otherwise, continue with Project 4.

INSIDE Stuff

Adding a new subfolder is like growing new branches on a tree. Subfolders sprout from existing folders or subfolders. If you want to create multiple layers of subfolders, first create the folders or subfolders that precede the ones you want to add.

If you try to read this floppy disk on a machine that doesn't have Windows 95, the folder names only have eight characters. Windows 95 automatically assigns the shorter DOS name by taking the first six characters of the long folder name, followed by a tilde (~) and a 1. If more than one folder name has the same six characters, the number after the tilde is incremented by one. For example, the folder names "Folder with a long name" and "Folder with a longer name" will appear as FOLDER~1 and FOLDER~2, respectively.

Summary

To	Do This
Open My Computer	Double-click the My Computer icon on the desktop.
Open a drive window	Double-click the drive icon in My Computer.
Open a folder window	Double-click a folder icon.
Cascade folder windows	Right-click the taskbar, then choose **C**ascade.
Tile folder windows	Right-click the taskbar, then choose Tile **H**orizontally or Tile **V**ertically.
Undo a tile or cascade arrangement	Right-click the taskbar, then choose **U**ndo Tile or **U**ndo Cascade.
Display large file icons	Choose **V**iew, Lar**g**e Icons.
Display small file icons	Choose **V**iew, S**m**all Icons.
Display files alphabetically	Choose **V**iew, **L**ist.
Display additional file information	Choose **V**iew, **D**etails.
Arrange files by name	Choose **V**iew, Arrange **I**cons, **N**ame.
Arrange files by type	Choose **V**iew, Arrange **I**cons, **T**ype.
Arrange files by size	Choose **V**iew, Arrange **I**cons, Si**z**e.
Arrange files by date	Choose **V**iew, Arrange **I**cons, **D**ate.
Select a folder or file	Click the folder or file icon.
Select adjacent folders or files	Click the first folder or file, hold down Shift, then click the last folder or file.
Select non-adjacent folders or files	Click the first folder or file, hold down Ctrl, then click the other folders or files.
Create a new folder	Open the drive or folder window where you want to create the folder. Choose **F**ile, Ne**w**, **F**older. Type the folder name, then press Enter.

Applying Your Skills

These "On Your Own" exercises enable you to practice the skills you have learned in this project. Take a few minutes to work through these exercises now.

On Your Own

Becoming Familiar with File Views in Windows 95 Folder Windows

1. In the My Computer window, double-click the hard drive icon (usually C:).
2. In the hard drive window, click the Windows folder icon.
3. Use the **V**iew menu to change the display to show the folder window in **D**etails view.
4. Use the **V**iew menu to arrange the files alphabetically by name.
5. Use the **V**iew menu to arrange the files alphabetically by type.
6. Change the display to Lar**g**e Icons, arranged by **N**ame.

Selecting Files

1. In the My Computer window, locate and open your hard drive (usually C:).
2. In the hard drive window, select the Windows folder.
3. Scroll down until you can see the file icons.
4. Select the first five files in the list.
5. Deselect the files.
6. Scroll through the folder window and select the following files: Accessories, Calc, Clock, and Control.
7. Return to your original desktop by closing all the windows you have opened.

Working with My Computer

1. Open My Computer. Double-click the drive C icon. From the folders shown, open the Windows folder. Then open the System folder.
2. Minimize the My Computer, drive C, and Windows folder windows in order to place them out of the way. Only the System folder window should be on the desktop. From its **V**iew menu, deselect the Status **B**ar and then reselect it. Notice the difference.
3. From the **V**iew menu, display the System folder contents by using Lar**g**e Icons, S**m**all Icons, **L**ist view, and **D**etails view.
4. Close the System folder window. Leave the My Computer, drive C, and Windows folder windows open. Click the Windows button on the taskbar to restore the Windows folder window.
5. Select the Cars file by clicking it. Note that the status bar shows the number and size of the object(s) selected.
6. Select the Castle Walls file. The Cars file is deselected.
7. Practice selecting adjacent files by clicking the Blue Rivets file. Hold down Shift and click the Bubbles file.
8. Select non-adjacent files by holding down Ctrl and clicking the Cars and Castle Walls files.

9. Continue to hold down Ctrl. Click on the scroll bar until the Mshearts file is shown. Select the file by clicking it. The status bar should indicate that three objects are selected. Close all open windows.

Creating Folders

1. Insert a disk in the floppy disk drive of your computer. Open My Computer and double-click the drive icon for the drive in which you inserted the floppy disk.
2. Choose **F**ile, **N**ew, **F**older from the menu bar. Name the new folder **Accounts**.
3. Double-click the Accounts folder to open a folder window for it. Create two new folders in the Accounts folder: **Accounts Receivable** and **Accounts Payable**.
4. Close all open windows.

Project 4

Managing Files

Objectives

In this project, you learn how to

- ➤ Copy Files
- ➤ Move Files
- ➤ Rename Files
- ➤ Delete Files
- ➤ Retrieve Deleted Files
- ➤ Format Floppy Disks

Why Would I Want To Do This?

In Project 3, you learned the basics of using My Computer. Now that you understand the My Computer window and how to customize it to meet your needs, you are ready to learn about managing your files. You can maintain your files and folders more easily with My Computer than with DOS commands. For example, instead of having to remember a long, cryptic DOS command to copy a file, you can click and drag the file to its new destination with the mouse.

Lesson 1: Copying Files

Copying files is an important part of keeping your work organized and secure. One of the most common reasons for copying files is security. The hard disk on which you store files is a mechanical device, and it has one of the highest failure rates among computer components. If your hard disk fails, the cost of replacing the disk is insignificant compared to the cost of the hours you worked creating the data on the hard disk. One way to prevent the loss of your data is to make a set of duplicate (or backup) files.

Other reasons why you might need to copy files include: taking a file home to work on it, sharing a file with a client or taking a file to a client's office, or transferring files back and forth between a desktop machine at the office and a notebook for travel.

When you copy or move files, you have a *source* and a *destination*. The source is the file(s) you want to copy. The destination can be a folder or a drive. Try copying files now.

Jargon Watch

A **source** is the file, folder, or drive that you want to copy. The **destination** is the location to which you want to copy a file, folder, or drive.

To Copy Files

1. **Open My Computer and double-click the drive C: icon.**

   Double-clicking a drive icon opens a window with the folders and files found on that drive. (If you need to review the steps to open My Computer, turn back to Lesson 1 in Project 3.)

2. **Scroll through the window and double-click the Sample Files folder.**

   Double-clicking the Sample Files folder icon opens a folder window showing files within the Sample Files folder.

3. **Choose View, Large Icons.**

   This step is optional. The larger icons are easier to drag and drop, so this setting is used here.

4 Insert a floppy disk into your floppy disk drive.

This can be the same floppy disk you used in Project 3. You will use this disk throughout this project as you learn how to copy, move, rename, and delete files.

5 Click the My Computer button on the taskbar.

Clicking the My Computer button moves the My Computer window up to the top of the stack so you can see the drive icons.

6 Double-click the floppy disk drive icon—for example, $3^1/_2$ Floppy (A:).

Double-clicking the floppy drive icon opens a window and displays the contents of the floppy disk. (If this is the same disk you used in Project 3, you will see the Loan Documents folder you created in Lesson 5 of that project.)

You should now have four windows open on the desktop: My Computer, the drive C: window, the Sample Files folder window, and the floppy drive folder window. The easiest way to copy files between different drives (or folders) is to tile the windows.

7 Right-click the taskbar and choose Tile Vertically.

The Tile command will arrange all open windows. Because there are four windows open, each window takes up a quarter of the desktop. Since you will be working with only two of the folder windows, the Windows window and the floppy drive window, you need to minimize the other two windows.

8 Click the Minimize button on the My Computer window; then click the Minimize button on the drive C: window.

Now that there are only two open windows, tile these two windows so that each takes up half the desktop.

9 Right-click the taskbar and choose Tile Vertically.

Your desktop should now look similar to Figure 4.1.

10 In the Sample Files folder window, click the Upgrader file.

Clicking a file selects it so you can take action on it. This approach follows the Windows philosophy of *select, then do.*

11 Drag the selected file over to the floppy drive folder window.

When you drag a file, a shadow of the file icon, called a drag-and-drop icon, moves with the mouse pointer (see Figure 4.2). Make sure you don't drag the file over the Loan Documents folder icon, or the file will be copied to that folder.

continues

To Copy Files (continued)

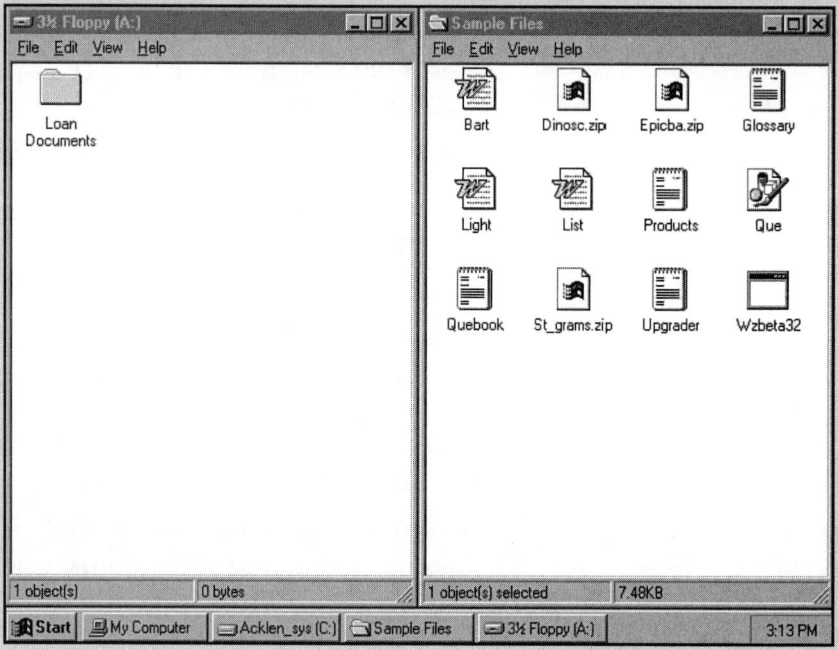

Figure 4.1
The two windows are tiled vertically.

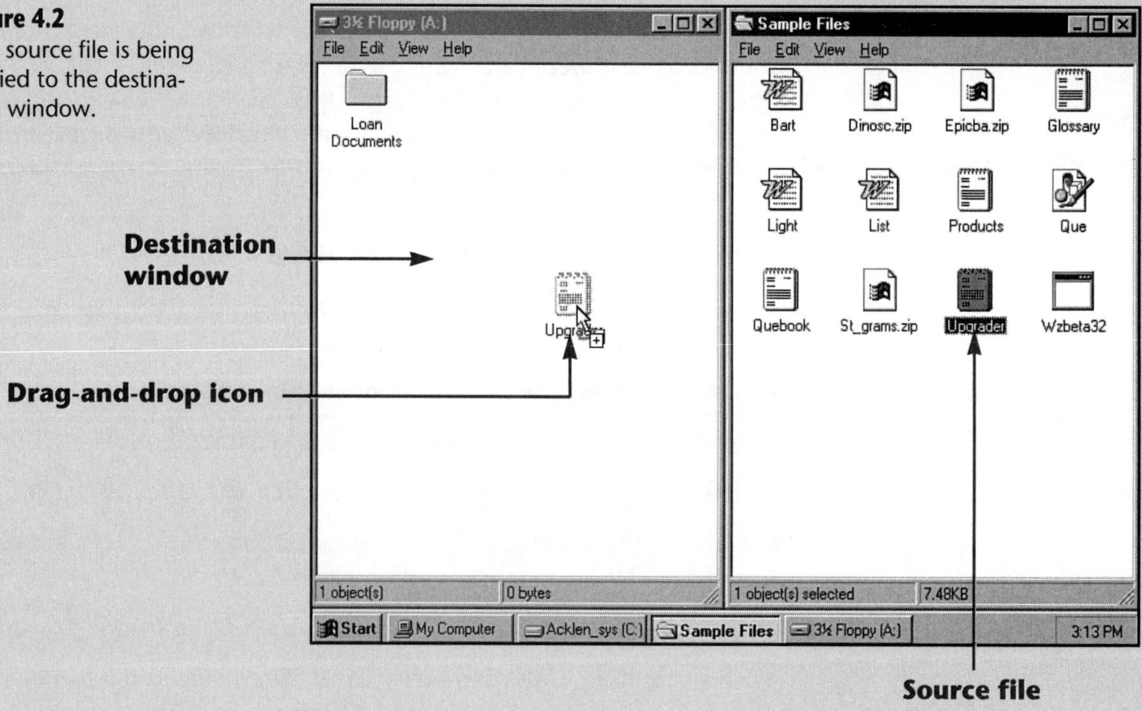

Figure 4.2
The source file is being copied to the destination window.

⑫ Release the mouse button.

Releasing the mouse button drops the file into the folder window for the floppy disk drive. When you drop the file into the new folder window, a Copying dialog box appears (see Figure 4.3). Windows animation shows pages flying out of one folder into another folder. The name of the file being copied appears in the lower-left corner, along with the names of the source and destination folders.

Figure 4.3
The Copying dialog box.

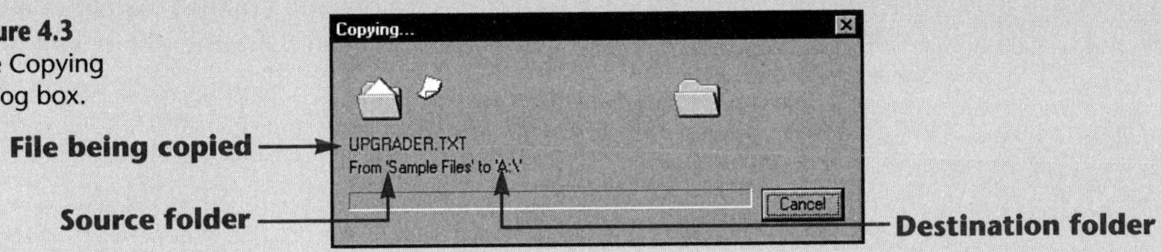

When the copy process is completed, the Copying dialog box closes, and the file appears in the floppy drive folder window (see Figure 4.4).

Figure 4.4
You have copied the Upgrader file to the floppy disk.

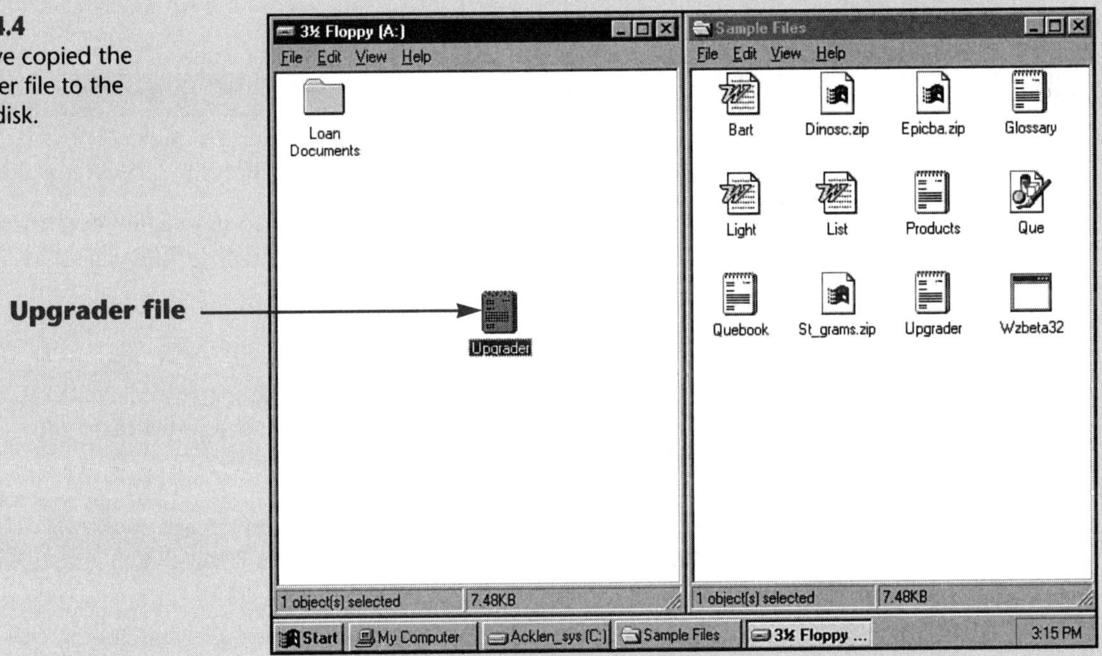

Leave the two folder windows open for the next lesson, where you learn how to move files.

If you change your mind, you can "undo" the file copy by choosing **E**dit, **U**ndo Copy.

Instead of using the mouse to drag copies of files to different folders, you can use menu commands to copy the files. You can use the **E**dit menu or the Context menu. First, select the file(s). Then, choose **E**dit or click the right mouse button. Choose **C**opy. Now, click in the destination folder window—this is where you want to copy the file. Choose **E**dit or click the right mouse button. Choose **P**aste.

If you need to move more than one file, click the first file, then hold down Ctrl as you click the other files. If you use the drag-and-drop technique, drag one of the selected files to the destination folder window; the rest of the selected files will follow.

If you click and drag a file from one disk drive to another, Windows automatically *copies* the file. If you need to copy a file in the same disk drive (for example, you want the file saved in two folders on the same drive), you can hold down Ctrl while you click and drag the file.

Lesson 2: Moving Files

You can move files just as easily as you can copy them. Moving a file places it in a new location and removes the original file from the old location. You can move files or folders to a new folder or drive. Moving a folder moves the entire contents: both the folder's files and any subfolders. Try moving files now.

To Move Files

1. **In the Sample Files folder window, click St_grams.zip file.**

   The St_grams file contains a program that will let you turn black-and-white bitmapped images into 3D Stereograms.

2. **Hold down Shift; then drag the file to the window for the floppy disk.**

   When you want to move a file by using the mouse, you need to hold down Shift before you drag. The drag-and-drop icon appears as it did when you copied a file (see Figure 4.5).

   If you have problems...

   Make sure you press and hold down Shift before you drag the file; otherwise, you will copy—not move—the file. Should this happen, right-click the folder window, and choose **U**ndo Copy. Then try again.

3. **Release the mouse button.**

   Releasing the mouse button drops the file into the folder window for the floppy disk. When you release the file, a Moving dialog box appears. This is the same dialog box you saw earlier when you copied the Upgrader file. Pay close attention to the title bars in these dialog boxes to confirm whether you are copying or moving a file.

   You should return the St_grams file to the Sample Files folder (so that the next class has it available to them), so move the file back now.

Figure 4.5
The source file is being moved to the destination folder window.

Drag-and-drop icon

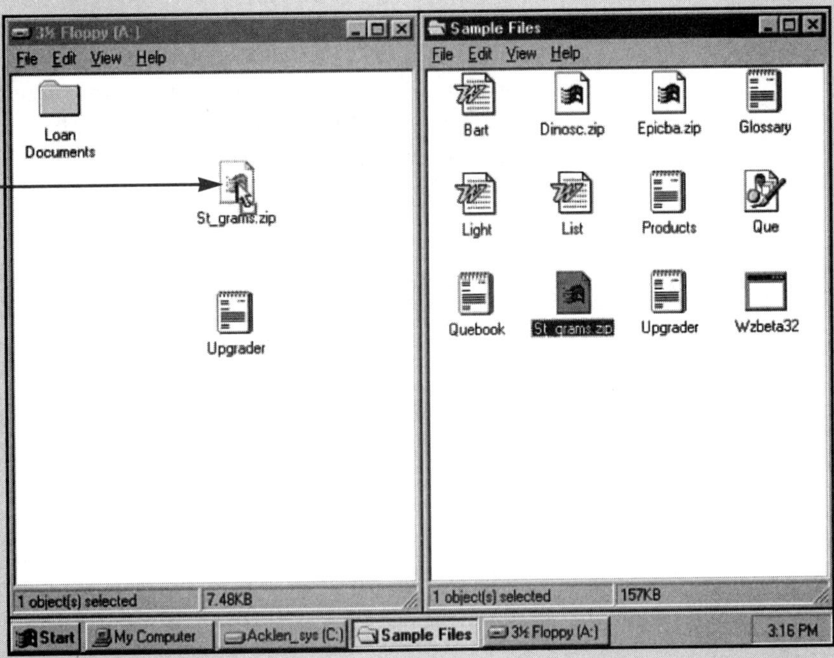

4. **Hold down ⇧Shift then click and drag the file over to the Sample Files folder window.**

5. **Release the mouse button.**

   The St_grams file now appears in the Sample Files folder window. Leave these two folder windows open for the next lesson, where you learn how to rename files.

If you change your mind, you can "undo" the file move by choosing **E**dit, **Un**do Move.

Instead of using the mouse to drag files to different folders, you can use menu commands to move the files. You can use the **E**dit menu or the Context menu. First select the file(s). Then choose **E**dit or click the right mouse button. Choose **M**ove. Now click in the destination folder window—this is where you want to move the file. Choose **E**dit or click the right mouse button. Choose **P**aste.

If you need to move more than one file, click the first file, then hold down Ctrl as you click the other files. Click one of the selected files and drag it to the destination folder window; the rest of the selected files will follow.

If you click and drag a file within the same disk drive, Windows automatically *moves* the file. If you need to move a file from one disk drive to another, you must hold down ⇧Shift while you click and drag the file.

Lesson 3: Renaming Files

Unless you do everything perfectly the first time, you will find times when you want to rename a file (or folder). The name you give a file when you create it might not seem appropriate three months later. Renaming a file is easy; all you have to do is select the file and then type a new name. Try renaming a file now.

To Rename Files

1 In the floppy disk folder window, point to the Upgrader file.

This is the file you copied from the Sample Files folder earlier in the project.

2 Click the right mouse button.

Clicking the right mouse button opens a Context menu of file-management commands that you can use on a selected file or a group of files (see Figure 4.6).

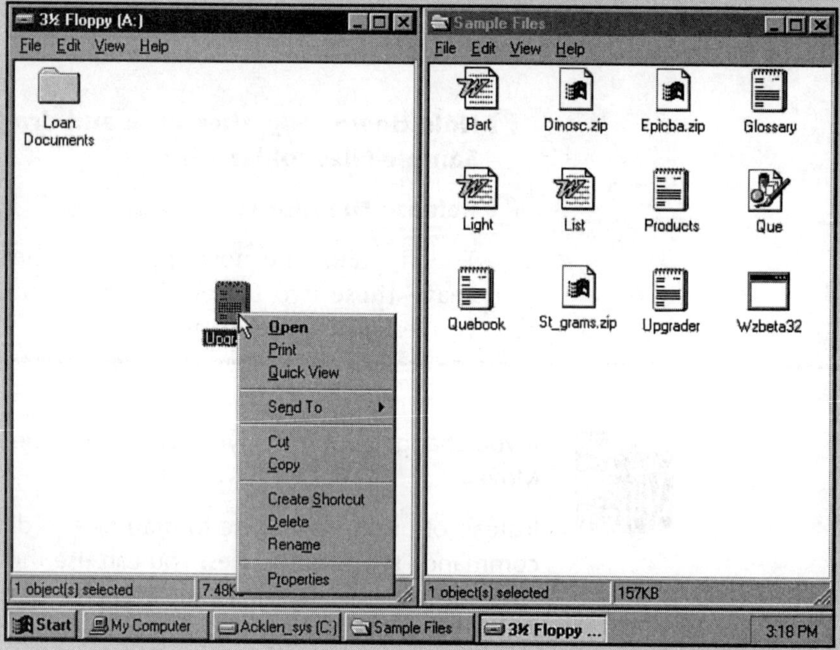

Figure 4.6
The Context menu for a selected file.

3 Choose Rename.

A box appears around the file name, and the file name is selected (see Figure 4.7). You can type a new name now, and it will automatically replace the selected text (the existing file name).

4 Type Upgrade Notes and press Enter.

The new file name now appears in the folder window under the file icon.

Leave these two folder windows open for the next lesson, where you learn how to delete files.

Figure 4.7
The existing file name is selected.

Selected file name

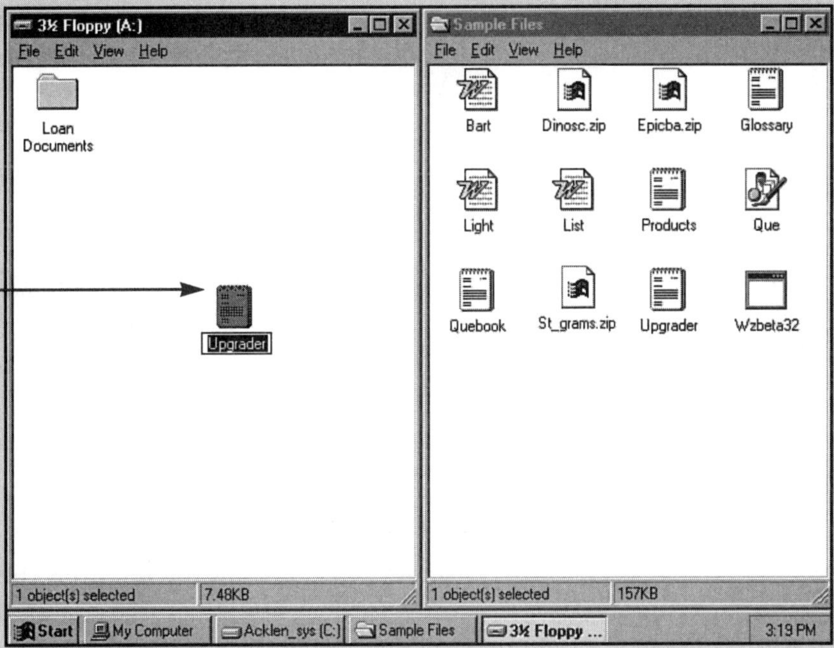

INSIDE Stuff

You can also click once on the icon, then click once on the icon name to rename an icon.

The steps to rename a folder are basically the same as those for renaming a file. Simply click the folder icon; then choose Rena**m**e from the **F**ile menu or the Context menu. Type a new folder name and press Enter.

If you change your mind, you can "undo" the file or folder rename by choosing **E**dit, **U**ndo Rename.

Lesson 4: Deleting Files

You can delete files or folders when you want to remove old work from your disk. Deleting excess files and folders makes more storage space available on the disk. If you choose to delete a folder that doesn't contain any files, it won't make much difference in storage space, but it will unclutter your drive. Now try deleting files.

To Delete Files

1 In the floppy disk folder window, click the file called Upgrade Notes.

This is the file you renamed in the preceding lesson. Delete the file from the floppy disk now.

continues

To Delete Files (continued)

2 Press Del.

The Confirm File Delete dialog box opens (see Figure 4.8). The message in this dialog box depends on the type of file you are deleting. If you were deleting a program file, the system would issue you a warning before deleting in order to safeguard your software.

Look again at the name of the file and the location to ensure that you really want to delete this file.

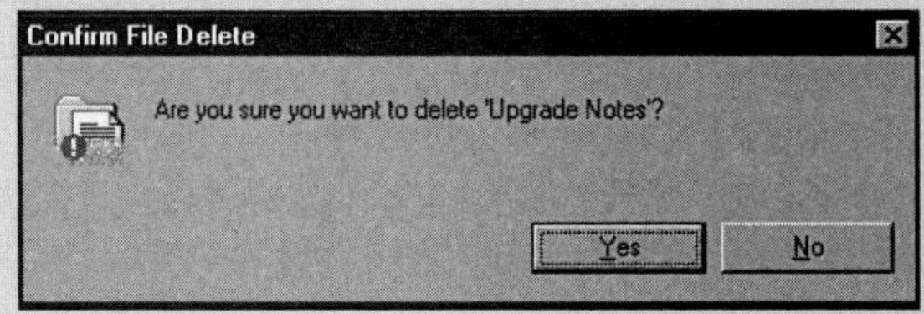

Figure 4.8
The Confirm File Delete dialog box.

3 Choose Yes.

Choosing **Y**es deletes the file from the floppy disk. The folder window for the floppy disk drive should be empty except for the Loan Documents folder you created earlier.

4 Click the Close button in the floppy drive folder window.

Clicking the Close button closes the folder window for the floppy drive window. Leave the Sample Files folder window open for the next lesson, where you learn how to retrieve deleted files.

INSIDE Stuff

If you change your mind, you can "undo" the deletion of a file or folder from your *local hard drive* by choosing **E**dit, **U**ndo Delete. You cannot choose these commands if you deleted a file or folder from a floppy disk.

If you aren't sure about deleting files or folders, move them to a floppy disk instead. This is called *archiving* and can save you a lot of time and trouble if you discover that you needed the files after all.

You can delete folders and subfolders by using the same steps you used to delete a file. If the folder (or subfolder) contains files or subfolders, the Confirm Folder Delete dialog box message will ask whether you want to delete the contents.

In the preceding lesson, you pressed Del to delete a file. You can also choose **D**elete from the **F**ile menu or the Context menu if you prefer.

Lesson 5: Recovering Deleted Files

It happens to everyone—you delete a file and then realize later that you really need it. In some cases, you can use the **U**ndo Delete command (discussed in the preceding "Inside Stuff" section) to recover a file. However, if you have performed another file action, such as renaming or moving a file, the **U**ndo Delete command is no longer available. The **U**ndo commands reverse only *the last action* taken on a file.

When this happens, you can recover the deleted file from the Recycle Bin. The Recycle Bin is a holding area for files you deleted from the hard disk. When you delete a file, Windows moves the file to the Recycle Bin, so the file isn't actually deleted from your hard disk until you clean out the Recycle Bin.

Try to recover a deleted file from the Recycle Bin now.

To Recover Deleted Files

1. **In the Sample Files folder window, click the St_grams file.**

   This is the same file you used earlier when you learned how to move files between folders. You will delete this file and then recover it from the Recycle Bin.

2. **Press Del.**

   The Confirm File Delete dialog box appears (see Figure 4.9). Because this file is located on a local drive (not a floppy drive), the message asks whether you are sure that you want to move the St_grams file to the Recycle Bin.

Figure 4.9
The Confirm File Delete dialog box.

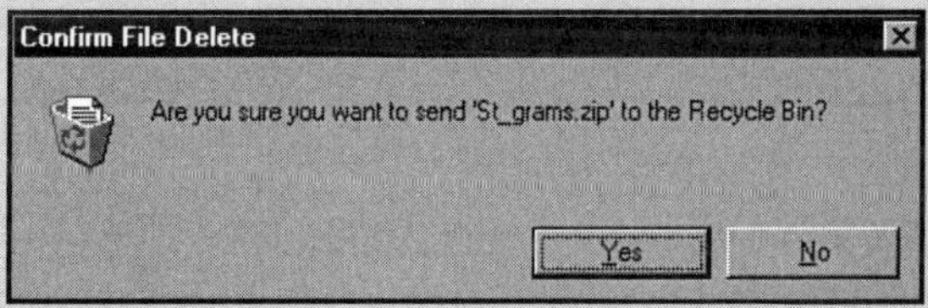

3. **Choose Yes.**

   Choosing Yes moves the file to the Recycle Bin. Recover the file now.

4. **Double-click the Recycle Bin icon on the desktop.**

   You might have to move the Sample Files folder window to find this icon. Double-clicking the Recycle Bin icon opens a window for the Recycle Bin (see Figure 4.10).

   The Recycle Bin contains the most recently deleted files at the top. The name and original location of the file are shown along with the date and time the file was deleted. The file type and size are also noted.

5. **Click the St_grams file.**

6. **Choose File, Restore.**

   The Restore command moves the St_grams file from the Recycle Bin back to the Sample Files folder. Switch to the Sample Files folder now.

continues

To Recover Deleted Files (continued)

Figure 4.10
The window for the Recycle Bin.

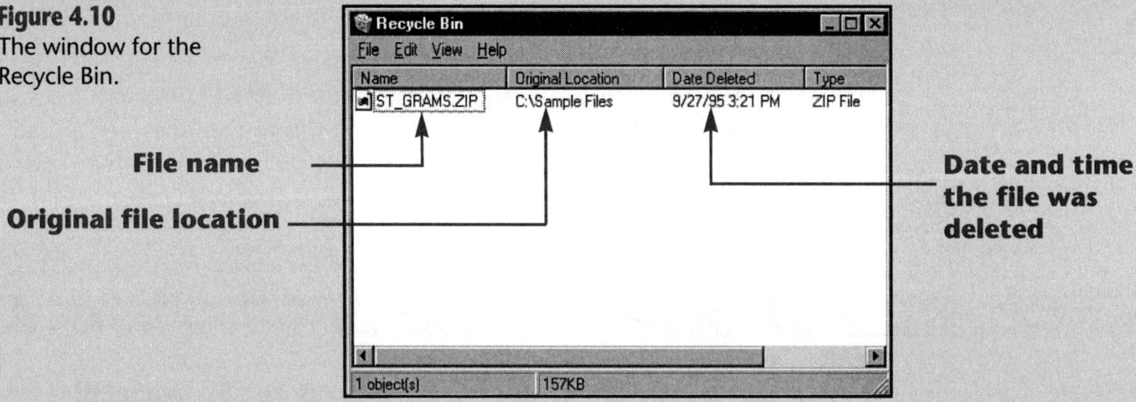

7 Click the Sample Files folder button on the taskbar.

Clicking the Sample Files folder button moves the Sample Files folder window to the top of the desktop. The St_grams file now appears in the Sample Files folder.

Close the Sample Files folder window, the Recycled window, and the drive C: window. My Computer is minimized, so the My Computer button should be the only button on the taskbar. Leave the desktop in this state for the next lesson, where you learn how to format floppy disks.

Because deleted files automatically move to the Recycle Bin, this is the first place you should go when you need to free up disk space. *Purging* or cleaning out the Recycle Bin physically removes the files from the hard drive, freeing up disk space.

The amount of space you have in the Recycle Bin depends on the amount of disk space in your computer and how much of that space has been allocated to the Recycle Bin. By default, 10 percent of your hard drive is reserved for the Recycle Bin.

In step 7 of the preceding tutorial, you used the **F**ile menu to select the R**e**store command. You can also right-click a file and then choose R**e**store from the Context menu that appears.

You can copy or move files in the Recycle Bin to locations other than the original location. Therefore, if you accidentally delete a file from one folder, you can move the file from the Recycle Bin to a different folder. You do this with the Cu**t** and **P**aste commands, not the R**e**store command. You can also drag and drop a file from the Recycle Bin to another window.

Lesson 6: Formatting Floppy Disks

When you buy new disks for storing files and folders, you cannot use the disks until you format them (some disks come already formatted).

Formatting prepares disks for use. Part of the process of formatting is to check for bad areas on a disk's magnetic surface. If any bad areas are found, they are identified so that data is not recorded there.

Capacity
The number of bytes that can be stored on a disk.

When you buy floppy disks, you need to know what *capacity* your disk drive uses. The capacity refers to the amount of information that can be stored on the floppy disk. There are two capacities for 5 1/4-inch floppy disks: low-density (which stores 360K of information or 360,000 characters); and high-density (which stores 1.2M [megabytes] or 1,200,000 characters). There are three capacities for 3 1/2-inch floppy disks: low-density (which stores 720K); high-density (which stores 1.44M); and extended-density (which stores 2.88M). Even though you can format a lower-density floppy disk in a higher-density drive, it is preferable to match disk capacities with your drive capacity.

To Format a Floppy Disk

1 Click the My Computer button on the taskbar.

Clicking the My Computer button opens the My Computer window on the desktop.

2 With the floppy disk still in the drive, click the floppy drive icon in the My Computer window.

Clicking the floppy drive icon selects the drive that contains the disk you want to format.

If you have problems...

Make sure you click the floppy drive icon only once. A single click selects the icon; a double-click opens a folder window.

3 Choose File, Format.

The Format dialog box appears (see Figure 4.11).

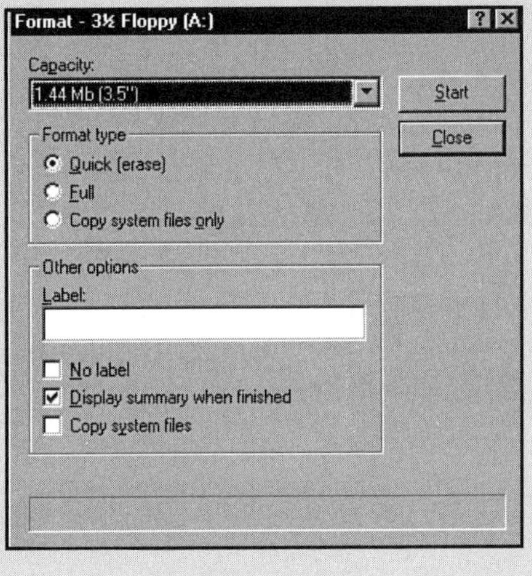

Figure 4.11
The Format dialog box.

continues

To Format a Floppy Disk (continued)

4 If necessary, select the appropriate disk capacity in the Capacity drop-down list box.

If you are unsure about the capacity of the floppy disk, take it out of the drive and look to see whether the capacity is noted on the disk. Otherwise, ask your instructor for assistance.

5 Choose Full in the Format type section.

This step isn't necessary if the **F**ull option is already selected. The Quick format option will only work on diskettes that have already been formatted.

6 Choose Start.

While Windows is formatting the disk, a progress indicator appears at the bottom of the dialog box. After your disk is formatted, a Format Results dialog box appears (see Figure 4.12). This dialog box reports the total amount of disk space (in bytes), how many bytes are used by system files, how many bytes are taken up by bad areas that are found, and how many bytes you have available on the disk.

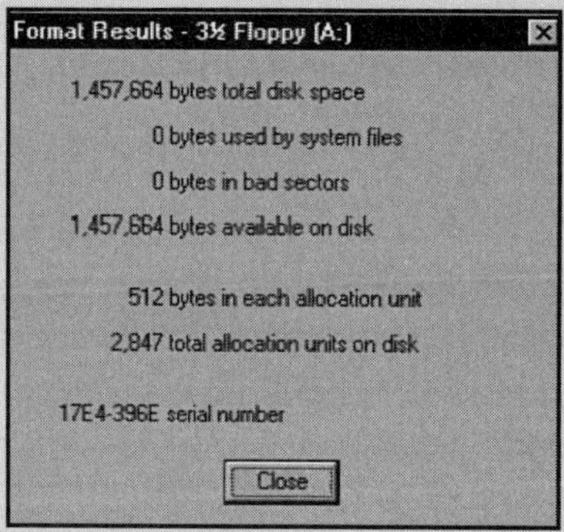

Figure 4.12
The Format Results dialog box.

7 Choose Close.

The format process is now complete, and the disk is ready to receive files.

If you have completed your session on the computer, shut down the Windows program before turning off the computer. Otherwise, continue with the "Applying Your Skills" section.

A good practice is to format an entire box of floppy disks at one time and then add a paper label to each formatted disk. That way, you know that open boxes of labeled disks are formatted disks.

In this lesson, you performed a full format on the disk. A quick format is faster, but can be done only on a disk that has been formatted before.

What Happens When You Use Your Disk Drives?

Copying, Moving, and Deleting Files

There are many reasons for *copying* files. You might want to give someone a copy of a file from your hard disk, so you copy it onto a floppy. Or you might want to work on rewriting a story, so you copy the original file under a different name; if you don't like the changes, you still have the original.

Moving a file happens less frequently. Generally, you move a file when you are organizing a disk and then realize that you want a file in a different folder. Or you might want to transfer a file from one disk to another.

Using 5.25-Inch Floppy Disks

The big black square floppy disk (or diskette) is getting rarer these days, but they once were the only type of PC disk available. Two varieties of 5.25-inch disks exist: double-density, and high-density. Double-density disks store up to 360K and can be read on any 5.25-inch drive. High-density disks can store up to 1.2M and can be read by any high-density drive (which includes most of the drives still in use). The only physical difference between the disk densities is that the magnetic coating on the high-density disk is more refined. A high-density disk can actually be formatted and used in a double-density drive, but then will hold only as much as a double-density disk.

You can accidentally wipe out information and make a disk unreadable by exposing it to a magnet. So keep your disks far away from magnets! You also should keep disks from bending and away from grit, grime, heat, and liquids.

Using 3.5-Inch Floppy Disks

The little 3.5-inch floppy disk might look like the 5.25-inch disk's kid brother, but if so, he's not only younger and smaller, but tougher and smarter as well. The well-protected disk stores anywhere from 720K for double-density disks (which define the low end), through the 1.44M high-density disks that most new machines can read and write, up to the extended-density 2.88M disks that are starting to be supported in advanced machines.

Using Hard Drives

When they were originally launched, the 5M to 10M storage capacity of hard drives seemed vast. Now, you would be hard pressed to find a new hard drive smaller than 40M. Most people buy hard drives that store hundreds of megabytes, and some store gigabytes (a gigabyte is 1,024 megabytes).

Hard drives are sometimes called *fixed disks* because the platters are fixed in place and designed not to be taken out of the drive. Some manufacturers now make removable hard disks; they generally involve sealed cartridges containing not only the platters, but also the read/write heads and other parts of the mechanism. Because hard disks are delicate, you should protect them from vibration or sudden impact, particularly while the computer is on and the disk is running.

For futher information relating to this topic, see Unit 2B, "Processing and Storage," of *Computers in Your Future*, by Marylin Meyer and Roberta Baber.

Summary

To...	Do This
Copy a file or files with **E**dit Menu	Open the folder that contains the Select the files you want to copyfile (or files). Choose **E**dit, **C**opy. Open the destination folder. Choose **E**dit, **P**aste.
Copy files with drag and drop	Open the source and destination folders. Arrange the two folder windows so you can see both of them. Select the file (or files) in the source window. Drag and drop the file(s) into the destination folder window.
Move a file or files with the **E**dit menu	Open the folder that contains the files you want to move. Select the file (or files). Choose **E**dit, **M**ove. Open the destination folder. Choose **E**dit, **P**aste.
Move files with drag and drop	Open the source and destination folders. Arrange the two folder windows so you can see both of them. Select the file (or files) in the source window. Hold down Shift, then drag and drop the file(s) into the destination folder window.
Rename a folder or file	Right-click the file or folder. Choose Rena**m**e. Type the new name, then press Enter.
Delete a folder or file(s)	Select the folder(s) or file(s). Press Del. Choose **Y**es to confirm the deletion.
Undo a file or folder operation	Choose **E**dit, then **U**ndo Move, **U**ndo Copy, or **U**ndo Rename.
Retrieve a deleted file or folder	Double-click the Recycle Bin icon on the desktop. Select the file(s) or folder(s). Choose **F**ile, R**e**store.
Format a floppy disk	Insert the disk in the drive. Open My Computer, then click the drive icon for the drive that contains the floppy disk. Choose **F**ile, For**m**at. Verify the capacity in the Ca**p**acity drop-down list box. Select the format type. Choose **S**tart.

Applying Your Skills

These "On Your Own" exercises enable you to practice the skills you have learned in this project. Take a few minutes to work through these exercises now.

On Your Own

Becoming Familiar with Moving and Copying Files

1. Insert a formatted disk into the floppy disk drive (usually A: or B:).
2. Open the Sample Files folder window as well as the floppy disk drive window. Tile them vertically.
3. Use the following methods to copy the indicated files from the Sample Files folder window to the floppy disk drive window:
   - Drag and drop the Bart file from the Sample Files folder window (the source folder) to the floppy drive folder window (the destination folder). When you are finished, you should see the file in both windows.
   - Click Que in the Sample Files folder window. From the menu bar, choose **E**dit, **C**opy. Click in the floppy drive folder window and choose **E**dit, **P**aste.
4. Move the Que file from the Sample Files folder window to the floppy drive folder window by using the following methods:
   - Hold down Shift and use the drag-and-drop technique to move the file from the Sample Files folder window to the floppy drive folder window. Then move the file back.
   - Select the Que file again. Right-click the mouse directly on the selected file. From the Context menu, choose Cu**t**. Right-click in the floppy drive folder window and choose **P**aste. The file is moved to the floppy disk drive.
   - Click the **E**dit menu in the floppy drive folder window and choose Cu**t**. Then click the **E**dit menu in the Sample Files folder window and choose **P**aste. The file moves back to its original location in the Sample Files folder.

Becoming Familiar with Copying and Renaming Files

1. Insert a formatted disk into the floppy disk drive (usually A: or B:).
2. In My Computer, open the Sample Files folder window as well as the floppy disk drive window.
3. In the Sample Files folder window, select the files Epicba (a file containing a pinball game) and Light (a file containing lightbulb jokes).
4. Copy these files to your floppy disk. Use the method you are the most comfortable with: click and drag, **E**dit menu, or Context menu.
5. Click the floppy drive button on the taskbar to move the floppy drive folder window to the top of the stack.
6. Select the Epicba file and rename it as **Pinball**.
7. Select the Light file and rename it as **Bulb**.

Becoming Familiar with Deleting and Undeleting Files

1. Delete the Bulb file from the floppy drive folder window.
2. Choose **E**dit, **U**ndo Delete to restore the deleted file.
3. Delete the Que file from the Sample Files folder window.
4. Confirm that you do, in fact, want to send the file to the Recycle Bin.
5. Recover the deleted file (Que.bmp) from the Recycle Bin.

Formatting Floppy Disks

1. Insert the disk used in the exercise on copying and renaming files into the disk drive.
2. In the My Computer window, click the drive icon representing the disk drive where the floppy disk is located.
3. Choose **F**ile, For**m**at to open the Format dialog box.
4. Choose the appropriate capacity from the Ca**p**acity drop-down list. Then perform a full format on the floppy disk.
5. Format the floppy disk again, this time using the quick format type. Notice how much faster the quick format is compared to the full format.

Project 5

Sharing Information

Objectives

In this project, you learn how to

- Copy and Paste Text in Windows Applications
- View and Save Data in the Clipboard
- Link Information between Programs
- Update LInked Information

Why Would I Do This?

Often, one program is better than another at handling certain kinds of information. Spreadsheets handle columns of numbers, do complicated analyses and calculations, and create graphs with ease. Drawing programs give you a lot of options for creating logos, importing pictures, and painting colorful graphics. Word processing programs provide many tools for formatting and assembling documents. However, real-world documents sometimes require combining these functions. You might need graphics in your annual report or sales figures in a newsletter.

One of the most useful features of Windows is its capability to run multiple programs at the same time and to transfer information between programs. Windows enables you to use different applications as if they were parts of a single program. By integrating programs, you multiply their power, making your work more efficient and your results more professional.

The following are some examples of uses for sharing information between programs:

- You can use mailing list information in a Windows database to set up a mail merge in a Windows word processing application.
- You can create sales projections, financial analyses, inventory reports, and investment analyses with Microsoft Excel or Lotus 1-2-3 for Windows, and then insert them into Windows word processing documents.
- You can link Microsoft Excel to a Windows database to monitor and analyze inventory.

This project teaches you how to copy and move text between applications by using the Windows Clipboard. You also learn how to establish links between programs so the information automatically updates when you make changes.

Lesson 1: Copying and Pasting Text in Windows Applications

Windows applications enable you to copy or move text in a document, from one document to a different document in the same application, or even to a document in a different Windows application. To give you this flexibility, Windows applications use the *Clipboard*, a temporary storage location that holds information in the computer's memory so you can copy or move information from one place to another. When you turn off your computer, the information in the Clipboard is automatically erased.

Almost all Windows applications contain the Cu**t**, **C**opy, and **P**aste commands on the **E**dit menu. These commands enable you to *cut* or *copy* information you select in one place, and then *paste* the information somewhere else. The process of copying and pasting between applications saves time, eliminates typing errors, and gives you the chance to use applications together as though they were part of a single application. Try copying a short section of text from the WordPad program to the Notepad program now.

To Copy and Paste Text in Windows Applications

1. **Using the Start button to open the Accessories menu, choose the WordPad application.**

   The WordPad application opens into a window on the desktop. Maximize the WordPad window to make it easier to see the text you will type.

2. **Click the Maximize button in the WordPad window.**

   If you recall, this is the middle button on the right side of the title bar. Clicking the Maximize button expands the WordPad window to fill the screen.

3. **Type the following:**

   To All Employees:

   Summer work hours will go into effect on June 1. Hours will be from 11:00am to 3:00pm. Enjoy your summer!

Your screen should now look like Figure 5.1.

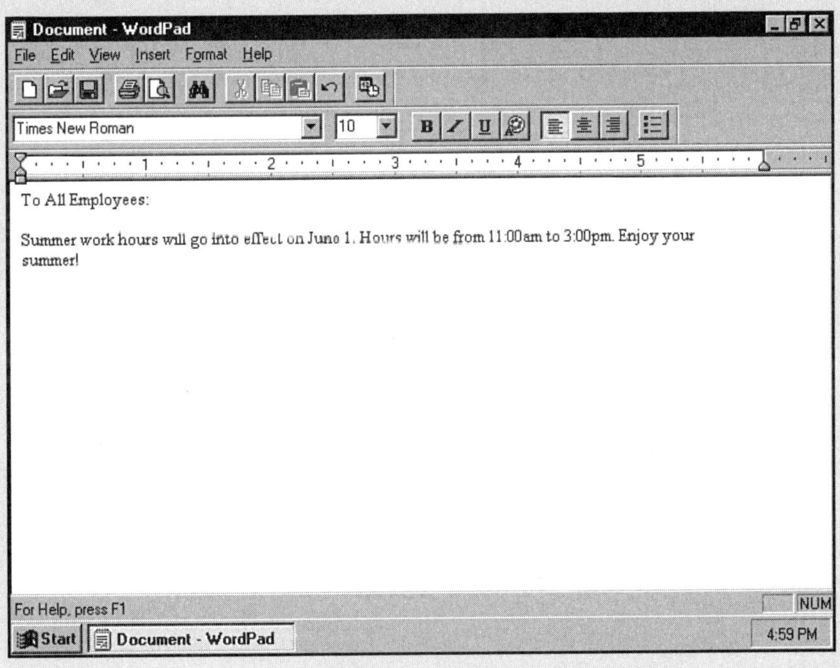

Figure 5.1
Sample text in the WordPad window.

4. **Position the mouse pointer at the top of the text.**

   When the mouse pointer is inside a document window, the pointer changes to an I-beam, which looks like a capital *I*. As noted in the preceding two projects, the basic operating philosophy in Windows is *select, then do*. This means you need to select what you want to work with before you can work with it.

continues

To Copy and Paste Text in Windows Applications (continued)

5 Click and drag the mouse pointer over the text until all the text is selected.

Selected text displays as white text on a black background, which is the opposite of unselected text; unselected text appears black on a white background. However, the colors might vary according to your setup in Windows. Your screen should look like Figure 5.2.

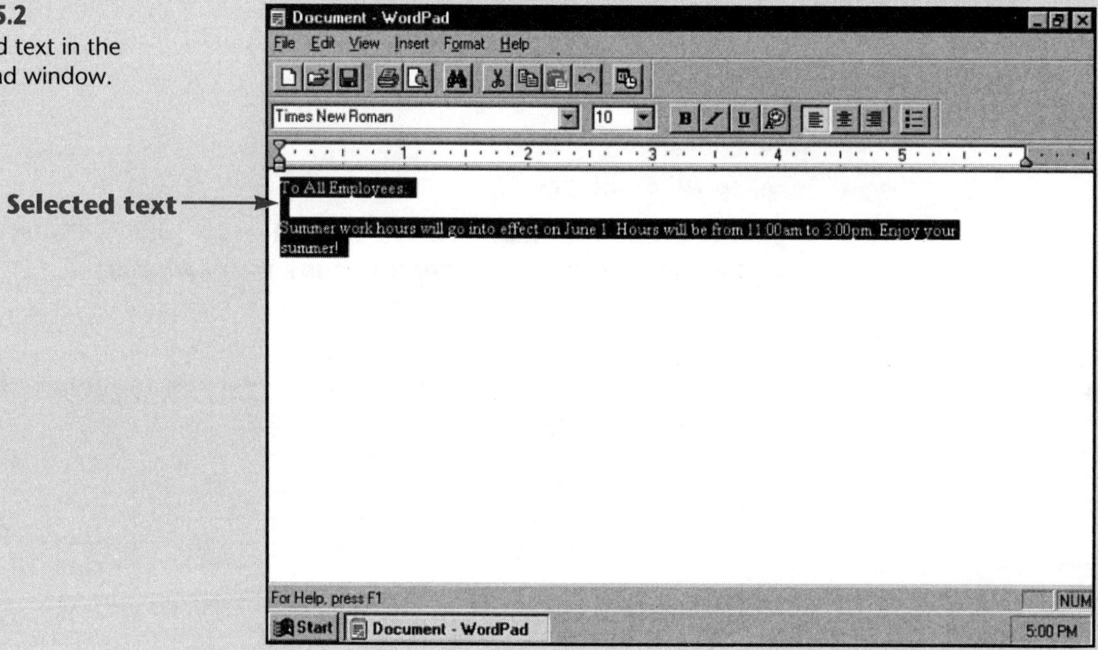

Figure 5.2
Selected text in the WordPad window.

6 Choose Edit, Copy.

A copy of the selected text is placed in the Windows Clipboard. You won't see the Clipboard on-screen; you have to use the Clipboard Viewer accessory program to view the contents of the Clipboard. This is covered in Lesson 2.

7 Using the Start button to open the Accessories menu, choose the Notepad application.

The Notepad application opens into a window on the desktop.

8 Choose Edit, Paste.

The text is copied from the Clipboard into the Notepad document (see Figure 5.3). Notice that the Notepad program uses a different font, so the text extends out to the right. As usual, a scroll bar is available if there is more information than will fit in the window.

Figure 5.3
The Notepad document has a copy of the pasted text.

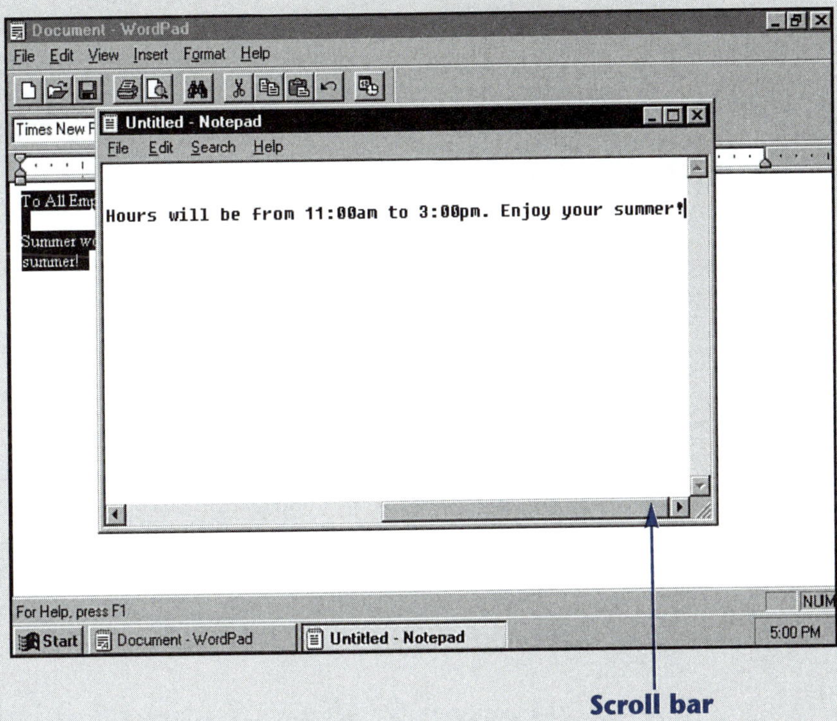

9. **Click the Close button in the Notepad window.**

   Clicking the Close button exits the Notepad program. When you exit a program without saving your changes first, a confirmation message box appears, asking whether you want to save the changes.

10. **Choose No.**

    Choosing **No** in the Notepad message box exits the program without saving the text you pasted into it.

11. **Click the Close button in the WordPad window.**

    A confirmation message box appears, asking whether you want to save the changes to the document. As in Notepad, it isn't necessary to save the document in WordPad. (These steps are intended for practice; ordinarily, you want to save your file before exiting a program.)

12. **Choose No.**

    The WordPad application closes without saving the sample text. Leave the desktop in this state for the next lesson.

Jargon Watch

The Windows **Clipboard** is a temporary storage area where material cut or copied from a document is stored until you paste the material. When you **cut** (or move) text, you remove selected text or graphics from an application and store the text or graphic in the Clipboard. When you **copy** text, you place a duplicate of the selected text or graphic into the Clipboard. When you **paste**, you insert information from the Clipboard into the active application at the current insertion point.

Shortcut keys are available for the Cu**t**, **C**opy, and **P**aste commands on the **E**dit menu. The shortcut for Cu**t** is Ctrl+X, the shortcut for **C**opy is Ctrl+C, and the shortcut for **P**aste is Ctrl+V.

The same steps you completed in this lesson are used for copying text between documents in the same application; the only difference is that, instead of switching to another application, you switch to another document. In addition, working with graphics is basically the same as working with text because you have to select a graphic before you can move or copy it.

Lesson 2: Viewing and Saving Data in the Clipboard

When you cut or copy information, Windows stores it in the Clipboard. The information stays in the Clipboard until you clear it or until you cut or copy new information. For this reason, you can paste the same item repeatedly until you clear or change the Clipboard.

Now try using the Clipboard Viewer application to view the contents of the Clipboard, save the Clipboard contents to a file, and retrieve a file into the Clipboard.

To View Clipboard Contents

1. **Using the Start button to open the Accessories menu, choose the Clipboard Viewer application.**

   The Clipboard Viewer window appears (see Figure 5.4). The last item you cut or copied is shown. In this case, it is the short section of text you copied from the WordPad window to the Notepad window in the last lesson.

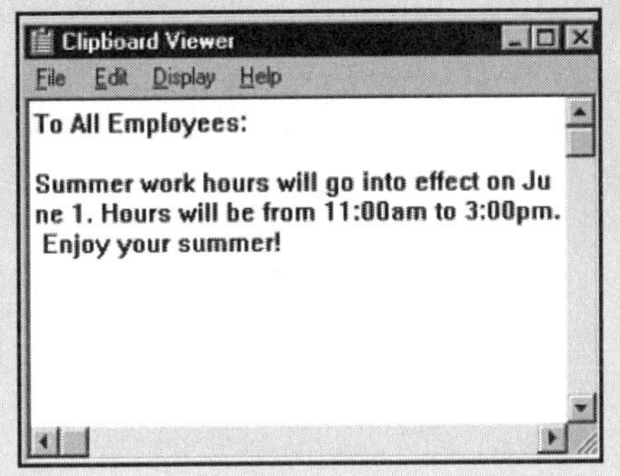

Figure 5.4
The Clipboard Viewer window shows the current contents of the Clipboard.

❷ Use the scroll bars to scroll through the window's contents.

The contents might look out of proportion in the Clipboard Viewer window, but they are adjusted after you paste them into the application.

❸ Choose File, Save As.

The Save As dialog box appears (see Figure 5.5).

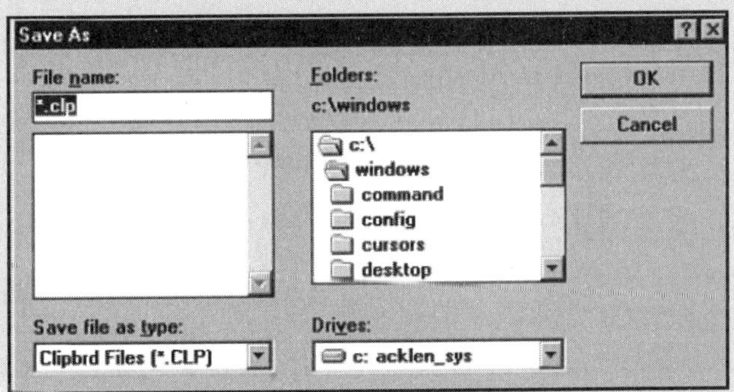

Figure 5.5
You use the Save As dialog box to save the Clipboard's contents.

❹ Type sample in the File name text box.

You can only use eight characters to name a file in the Clipboard Viewer program.

❺ Choose OK.

Now that you have saved the sample text to a file, you can retrieve it to the Clipboard whenever you need the text again.

❻ Choose File, Open.

The Open dialog box appears (see Figure 5.6). Notice that the Clipboard Viewer program automatically assigned a CLP extension when you saved the file.

continues

To View Clipboard Contents (continued)

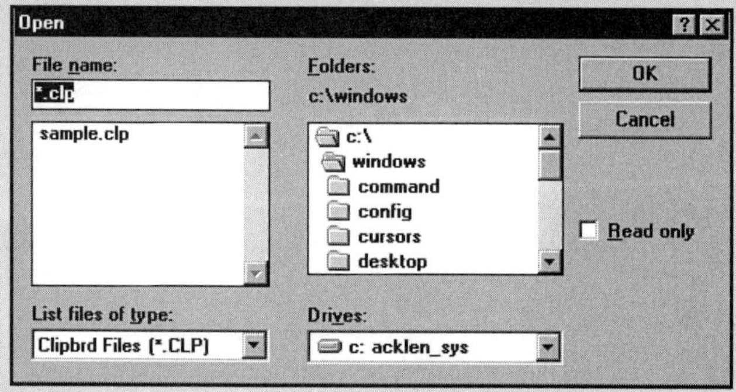

Figure 5.6
You use the Open dialog box to open a Clipboard file.

7 Double-click Sample.clp in the File name list box.

Double-clicking a file in a list box opens the file—in this case, the SAMPLE.CLP file—in the Clipboard Viewer window. A dialog box appears, confirming that you want to clear the contents of the Clipboard.

8 Choose Yes.

Choosing **Y**es clears the current contents of the Clipboard and opens the file into the Clipboard Viewer window. Because the contents of the Clipboard and the contents of the file are the same, you won't notice any difference in the Clipboard Viewer.

9 Click the Close button in the Clipboard Viewer window.

This action closes the Clipboard Viewer window. Leave the desktop in this state for the next lesson.

Lesson 3: Linking Information between Programs

The procedure for copying and pasting information from the Clipboard has limitations. When you copy and paste information, there is no enduring tie between the *source* and *destination* documents. If you make a change in the source document, you must either make the same change in the destination document to keep it current, or repeat the copy-and-paste operation so you can paste the most current version of the text. Either way, you must repeat an action. With object linking and embedding, called *OLE*, you can create a connection between the source and destination documents.

When you create a *link* between documents, a connection is created. If you make changes to the information, the link automatically updates the information, so both the source and destination documents are always up-to-date.

When you *embed* information from the source document into the destination document, the source information actually becomes a part of the destination document. You can then modify the destination document without affecting the information in the source document, and vice versa. Try to create a link now.

Jargon Watch

A **link** is a reference from within a destination document to information in a source document. A **source** is a document or application supplying linked information. A **destination** is a document or application receiving linked information.

To Link Information between Programs

1 Using the Start button to open the Accessories menu, choose the WordPad application.

2 Type the following text:

Grant,

I found this file, called Que, with all the sample files. I would like to use it in our training classes.

Then press ↵Enter twice.

Your screen should look like Figure 5.7.

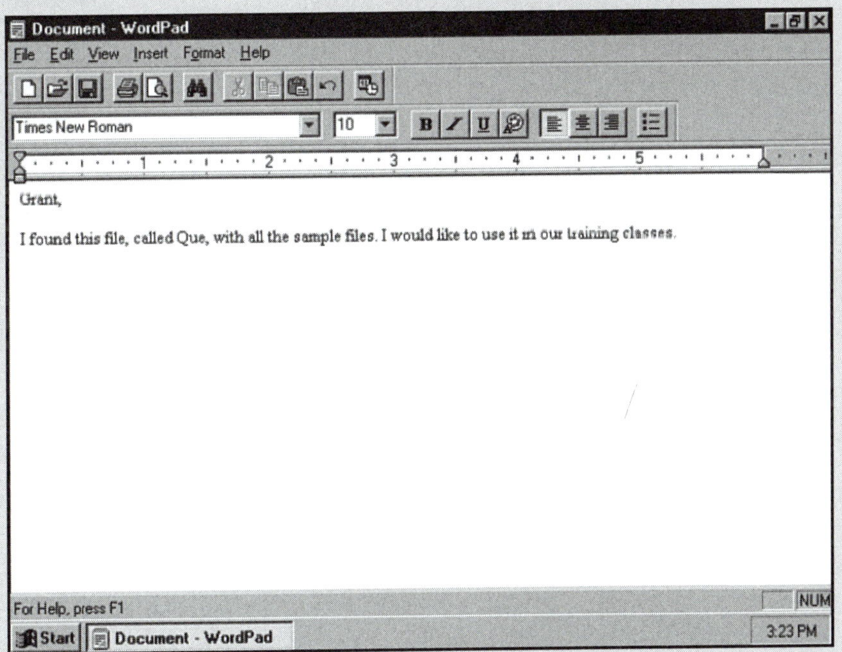

Figure 5.7
The sample text in the WordPad window.

3 Choose Insert, Object.

The Insert Object dialog box appears. The Object **T**ype list box contains a list of objects you can insert in a WordPad document.

continues

To Link Information between Programs (continued)

4 Click the Create from File option button.

When you choose Create from **F**ile, the Object **T**ype list box is replaced by the Fil**e** text box. You need to choose Create from **F**ile if you want to use a file already saved to disk. If you want to create an image from scratch, choose Create **N**ew.

5 Select `C:\WINDOWS\`, press Delete, type C:\, click on Browse, and select Que.

Notice that the file name has a BMP at the end. This three-letter file extension stands for *bitmap*. The QUE file is a bit-mapped graphic image, which means the image is formed by an intricate pattern of dots. Bitmapped images are produced by paint programs, such as Windows 95 Paint. The dialog box should now look like Figure 5.8.

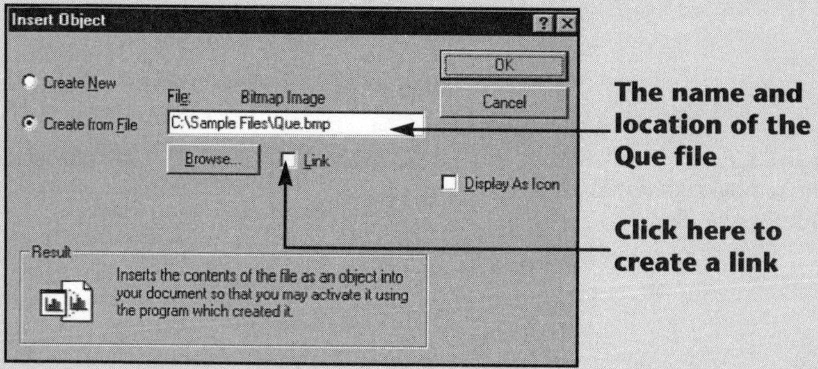

Figure 5.8
The Insert Object dialog box.

If you have problems...

If you get an error message that the file cannot be found, make sure you typed the name and location of the file exactly as it appears in step 5. You can click the **B**rowse button to open the Browse dialog box, which you can use for looking for the file. If you aren't sure where the Windows files are stored, ask your instructor for assistance.

6 Click the Link check box.

This creates a link between the file and the WordPad document. If you make changes to the Que file later, they are reflected automatically in the document.

7 Choose OK.

The picture is inserted at the end of the document—which is where the insertion point was located—and the link is created. Your screen should now look like Figure 5.9.

Figure 5.9
The QUE file is now linked to the WordPad document.

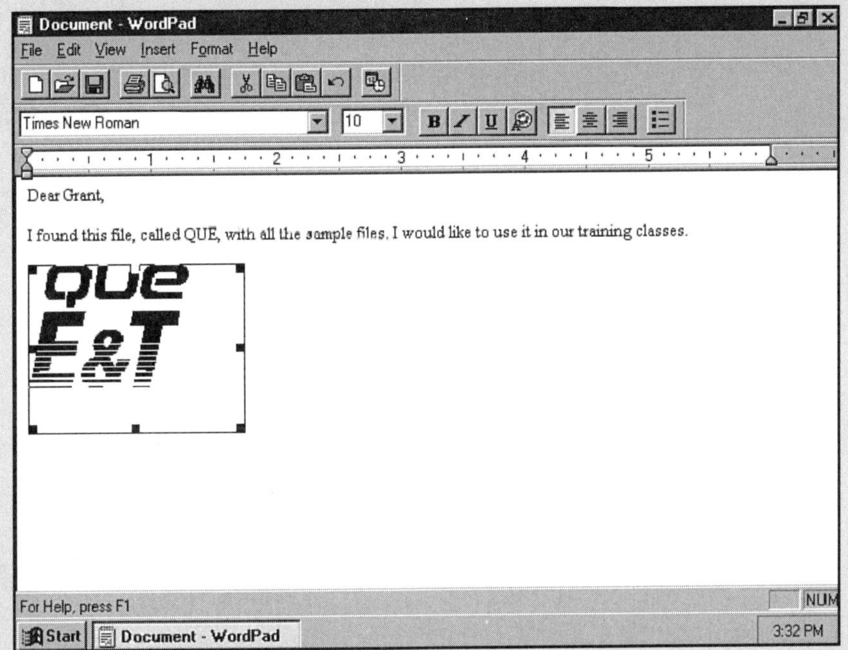

Leave the WordPad window open for the next lesson, in which you learn how a link actually works.

With *object linking and embedding (OLE)*, you can insert objects from other applications into your documents. These objects are linked to their originating application (the application they are created or edited in), so you can edit an object from within any application. You don't have to switch to the original application—OLE takes care of that for you.

When you insert a linked object, you really insert a link to the object's file. If you make changes to the object (from any application) and save them to the object's file, the changes are automatically reflected in every document that contains that object.

When you insert an embedded object, the object becomes a part of that document. When you edit the object from within this document, the changes are reflected only in this document—they will not affect other documents containing the object.

Lesson 4: Updating Linked Information

After you create a link, you can modify the source information in the originating application and have those changes reflected in the destination document. In Lesson 3, you created an automatic link between the WordPad document and the picture in the Paint window. Now try modifying the picture in Paint and watching the changes automatically reflected in the WordPad document.

To Update Linked Information

1 Double-click the Que picture.

Double-clicking the picture starts the Paint application and opens the Que file (see Figure 5.10).

You might want to take a minute now to arrange the two windows so you can see the upper half of the Que picture in both the WordPad window and the Paint window. This arrangement makes it easier for you to see the link automatically update the picture in the WordPad window as you make your changes.

Figure 5.10
The Que file is open in the Paint window.

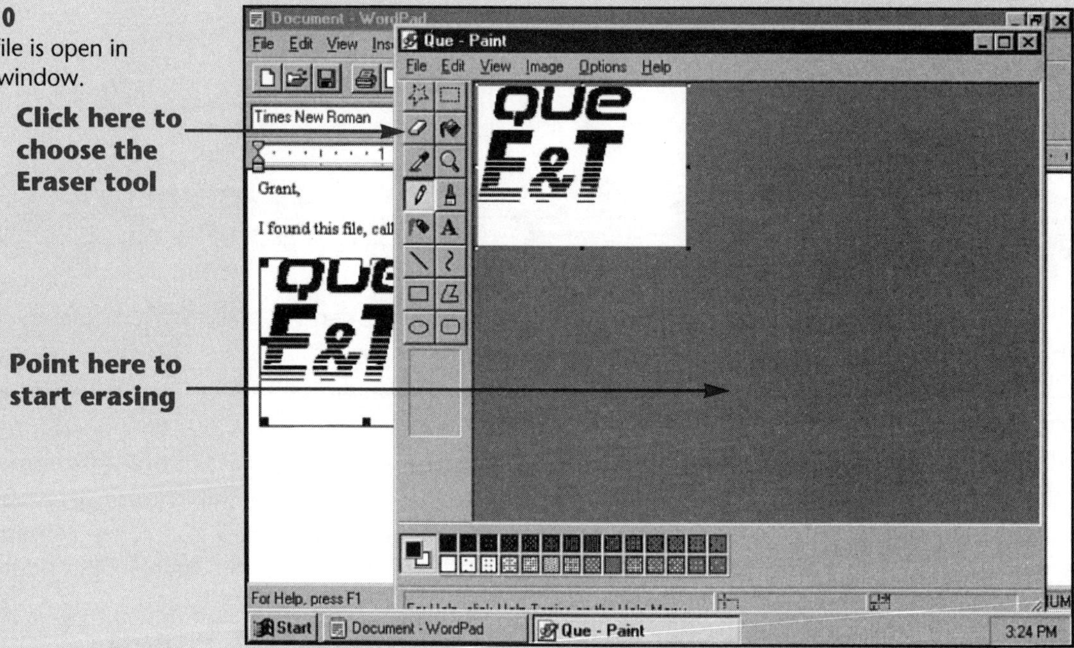

2 Click the Eraser tool.

Clicking the Eraser tool enables you to erase portions of the image in the Paint window (see Figure 5.10).

3 Move the pointer to the middle of the Que picture.

See Figure 5.10 for the approximate position—this is where you want to erase part of the picture. The mouse pointer changes to a small square.

4 Click the mouse button, then drag the pointer back and forth.

Dragging the pointer across the picture erases that part of the picture.

5 Release the mouse button.

Releasing the mouse button stops the erasing process and updates the picture in the WordPad window (see Figure 5.11).

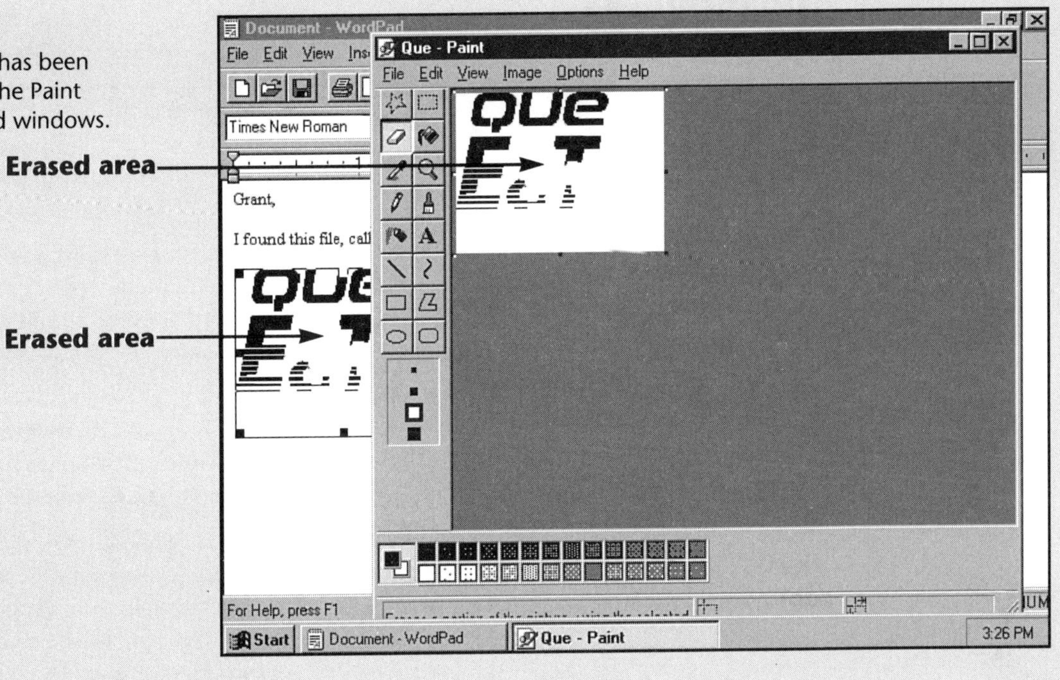

Figure 5.11
The Que file has been modified in the Paint and WordPad windows.

6 Click the Close button in the Paint window.

A Paint message box appears, asking whether you want to save the changes you made. Because you have just been practicing with the Que file, it isn't necessary to save the changes. In a real situation, after you modify a linked file, you must save the changes.

7 Choose No.

Choosing **N**o in the Paint message box exits the Paint application without saving the changes.

8 Click the Close button in the WordPad window.

A WordPad message box appears, asking whether you want to save the changes you have made. Because you have just been practicing with the sample text, it isn't necessary to save the changes.

9 Choose No.

Choosing **N**o in the WordPad message box exits the WordPad application without saving the changes.

If you have completed your session on the computer, shut down the Windows program before turning off the computer. Otherwise, continue with the "Applying Your Skills" section.

Summary

To	Do This
Copy and paste text in Windows programs	Select the text you want to copy. Choose **E**dit, **C**opy. Switch to the program where you want to paste the text. Choose **E**dit, **P**aste.
View the contents of the Clipboard	From the Start menu, open the Accessories menu, then choose the Clipboard Viewer. Use the scroll bars to scroll through the window's contents.
Save the contents of the Clipboard	From the Clipboard Viewer window, choose **F**ile, Save **A**s. Type a short file name (eight letters or less) in the File **N**ame text box. Choose OK.
Open a Clipboard file	From the Clipboard Viewer, choose **F**ile, **O**pen. Double-click a clipboard file from the File **N**ame list box to open the file. Choose **Y**es to clear the current contents of the Clipboard, or No if you want to save the contents of the Clipboard before you clear it.
Insert an object in a file	Open the Windows program. Position the insertion point where you want the object to appear. Choose **I**nsert, **N**ew Object. Click the Create from **F**ile option button. Select the text in the File text box, then type the name and location of the file; or, click the Browse button to look for the file. Click the **L**ink check box if you want to create a link to the object; deselect the **L**ink check box if you want to simply embed the object in the document.
Edit a linked object	Double-click the object in the destination document. The source application starts and the object file opens. Make your changes. Close the source application and save your changes to the object file.
Edit an embedded object	Double-click the object in the destination document. The source application starts and the object file opens. Make your changes. Close the source application. When you close the destination document, save your changes to the document.

Applying Your Skills

These "On Your Own" exercises enable you to practice the skills you have learned in this project. Take a few minutes to work through these exercises now.

On Your Own

Copying and Pasting in a Document

1. Use the Start menu to start the WordPad program.
2. Type the following:

   = = = = = = = = = = = = = = = = = = =
   1996 Spring Schedule

3. Select the line with the series of equal signs.
4. From the **E**dit menu, choose **C**opy.
5. Position the insertion point on a blank line underneath the line `1996 Spring Schedule.`
6. Choose **E**dit, **P**aste.
7. Select the heading (all three lines).
8. Choose **E**dit, **C**opy.
9. Press ↵Enter several times to insert blank lines.
10. Choose **E**dit, **P**aste. You should now have two complete sets of heading information.
11. Close WordPad without saving the changes you made in the document.

Becoming Familiar with the Clipboard Viewer

1. Using the Start menu, open the Clipboard Viewer application. The heading you copied in the last exercise is still in the Clipboard, so it appears in the Clipboard Viewer window.
2. Save the heading text with the name Heading. You cannot assign a long file name in the Clipboard Viewer program, so you have to use a name with either eight or fewer letters. The Clipboard Viewer automatically assigns the CLP extension so it can identify the file as a Clipboard file later.
3. Choose **E**dit, **D**elete to clear the contents of the Clipboard.
4. Open the Heading file you saved earlier back into the Clipboard Viewer window.
5. Close the Clipboard Viewer program.

Copying and Pasting between Applications

1. Use the Start menu on the taskbar to access **P**rograms, Accessories, Calculator.
2. Using the mouse, click the Calculator buttons to multiply 47 by 20. (that is, click 47, *, 20, and =).
3. From the **E**dit menu, choose **C**opy. Close the Calculator application.
4. Start the WordPad program and type the following sentence:

   The cost of sending 20 employees to Windows 95 training will be $47 each. The total cost is
5. From WordPad's **E**dit menu, choose **P**aste. The information that was placed in the Clipboard earlier is now pasted into your WordPad document.
6. Close WordPad without saving the file.

Becoming Familiar with Object Linking and Embedding

1. From Accessories, open WordPad and type the following letter:

   Dear Jillian:

   I have been using Windows 95 and really love the object linking and embedding feature! With it, I can open a program and link it to another file or program.

   Sincerely,
2. Move the mouse pointer below the letter's closing and choose **I**nsert, **O**bject from the menu.
3. From the Object **T**ype list, choose Paintbrush Picture and click OK. When you click OK, the Paint program opens within WordPad.
4. Click the Pencil icon on the Toolbar and then, using the mouse, write your name.
5. Click outside the box containing your name. The paint object is embedded in your WordPad document.
6. Double-click your name. The Paint program reopens, giving you the opportunity to make revisions.
7. Click the Eraser icon on the Toolbar. Using the mouse, erase your name.
8. Click a color from the palette and then click the Pencil icon on the Toolbar.
9. Rewrite your name and then click outside the box to embed the drawing within WordPad.
10. Close WordPad without saving the file.

Project 6

Customizing Windows

Objectives

In this project, you learn how to

- Change the Screen Saver
- Customize the Desktop
- Reset the Date and Time
- Change Mouse Settings
- Add Shortcuts to the Startup Folder
- Print a File
- Use the Print Manager

Why Would I Do This?

One of the advantages of working in the Windows environment is that you can customize many areas of the program to meet your needs. Some of the changes you can make are purely aesthetic, but others can help improve your productivity. This project focuses on the areas most often customized. You learn how to change the screen saver, wallpaper, and pattern for the desktop. You learn how to reset the system clock and how to fine-tune the mouse settings. You also learn how to add icons to your Startup folder so the items you use frequently open automatically when you start Windows. Finally, you learn how to print a file from a Windows application and how to use the Print Manager to manage your print jobs.

Lesson 1: Changing the Screen Saver

Screen saver
A utility program that prolongs the life of your monitor by changing the screen display.

If you are away from your computer for a period of time, a screen saver appears on your screen. A *screen saver* is a utility program that changes the screen display to prevent your monitor from being damaged by images that are continuously displayed on-screen when your computer remains idle for a period of time. Although newer monitors really aren't subject to "burn in," screen savers can provide so much enjoyment that most people use them anyway. In Windows, the screen saver is turned off by default.

If you decide to use a screen saver, you can choose which screen saver to display and the length of time the keyboard must be idle before the screen saver appears. If you choose the Marquee screen saver, you can type your own text to appear across the screen. This is helpful if you are going to be in a meeting and want to leave a message for anyone who stops by your desk. Try changing the screen saver now.

To Change the Screen Saver

1. **Right-click the desktop.**

   Right-clicking the desktop opens the Context menu for the desktop (see Figure 6.1).

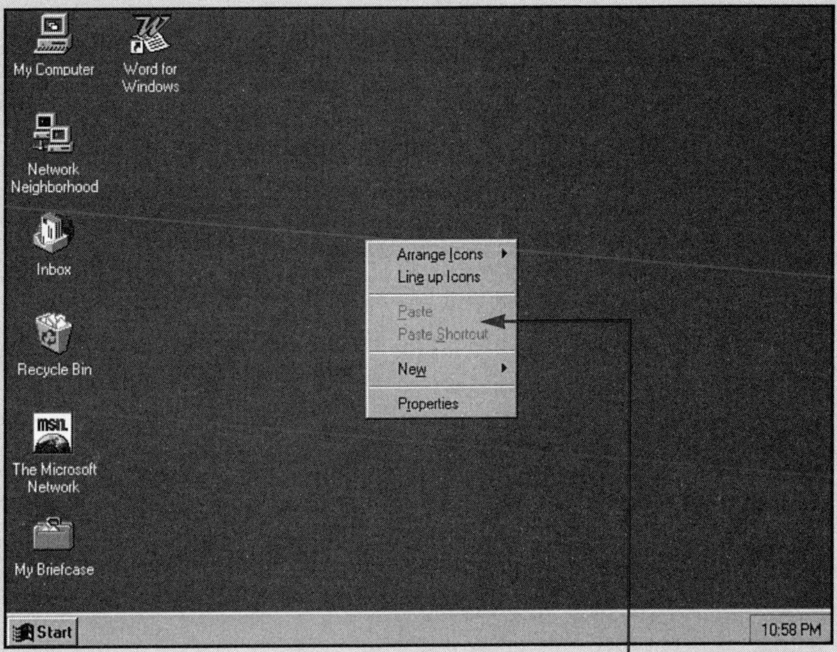

Figure 6.1
A right-click on the desktop opens the desktop Context menu.

Desktop Context menu

❷ Choose Properties.

Choosing Properties opens the Display Properties dialog box (see Figure 6.2). The four tabs at the top of the dialog box identify the different pages in the dialog box.

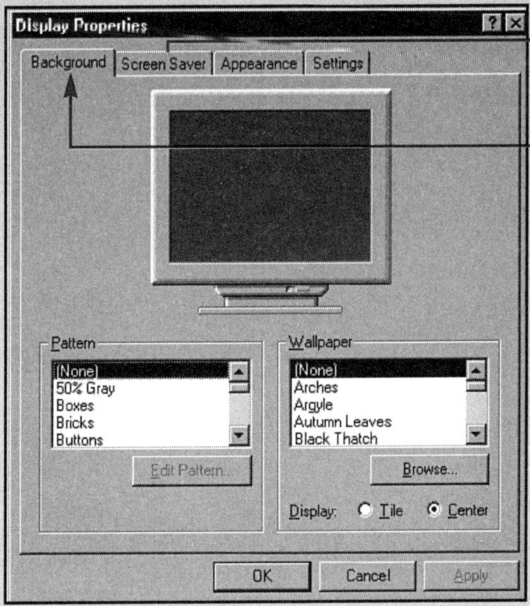

Figure 6.2
The Display Properties dialog box.

Click here to change the screen saver

Click here to change the background

❸ Click the Screen Saver tab.

The Screen Saver page moves to the front (see Figure 6.3).

continues

To Change the Screen Saver (continued)

Figure 6.3
The Screen Saver page.

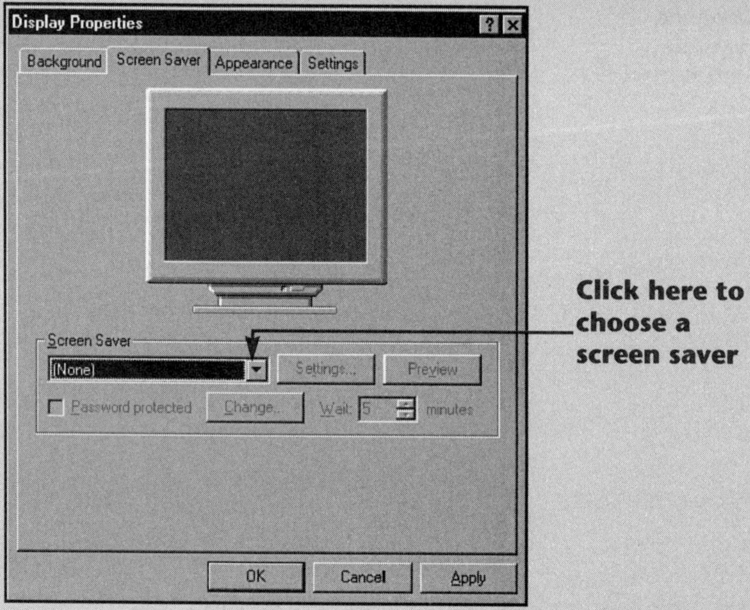

❹ **Click the Screen Saver drop-down list arrow.**

This opens a list of screen savers that come with the Windows program.

❺ **Choose Scrolling Marquee.**

The **S**creen Saver list box now displays `Scrolling Marquee` as the screen saver. The sample screen shows you how Scrolling Marquee is currently set up. The current message appears in red on a black background. You can change the message and the colors to suit you.

❻ **Click the up or down scroll arrow button in the Wait box to choose 3 minutes.**

This is the delay time—the amount of time the keyboard has to be idle before the screen saver comes on.

❼ **Choose Settings.**

Choosing Se**t**tings opens the Options for Scrolling Marquee dialog box (see Figure 6.4). Type your own short message now.

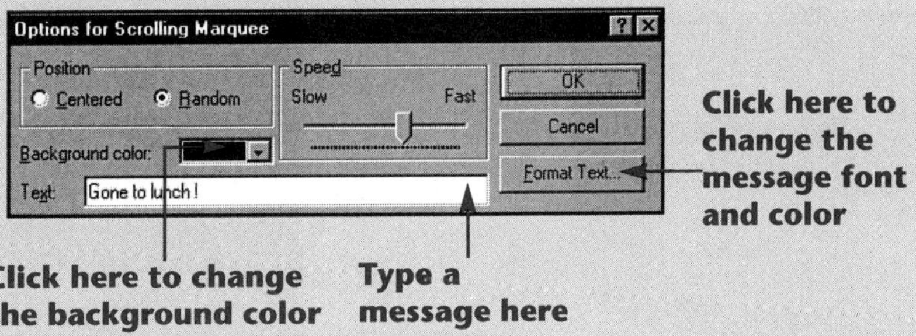

Figure 6.4
You can customize the Scrolling Marquee screen saver in the Options for Scrolling Marquee dialog box.

8. **Select the text in the Text text box and type Don't go away - I'll be right back!**

   This is the message you want to scroll across your screen while you are away from your desk.

9. **Choose OK.**

   Choosing OK saves your changes and takes you back to the Display Properties dialog box. The sample screen now shows your message scrolling across the desktop.

10. **Click the Preview button.**

    This activates the screen saver so you can see how it will look.

11. **Press any key or move the mouse to return to the Display Properties dialog box.**

    Pressing a key or moving the mouse turns off the screen saver. Leave the Display Properties dialog box open for the next lesson, in which you learn how to change the pattern and wallpaper.

Lesson 2: Customizing the Desktop

Pattern
A design you can display across the desktop.

Wallpaper
A graphic (or picture) file you can display on your desktop.

If you don't like the solid color that appears on your desktop when you open Windows, you can customize the appearance of the desktop by changing the *pattern* or *wallpaper*. Using a graphic or picture as the Windows desktop is a nice personal touch. Furthermore, Windows comes with a collection of graphics for the desktop. Try your hand at customizing the desktop now.

To Customize the Desktop

1 In the Display Properties dialog box, click the Background tab.

Clicking the Background tab switches to the Background page (see Figure 6.5). This is the page you see first when you open this dialog box.

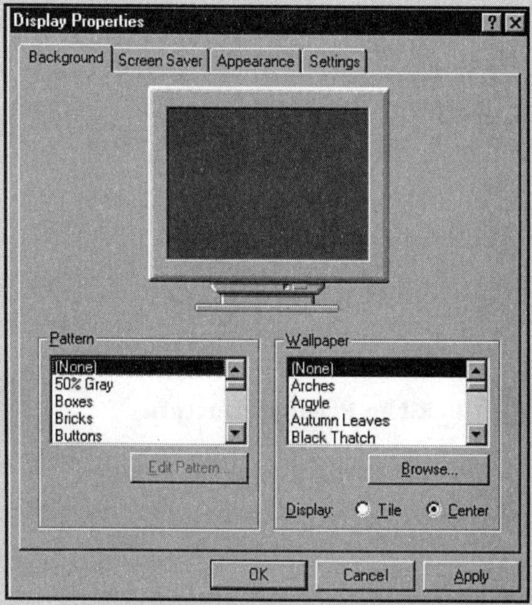

Figure 6.5
You use the Background page to choose a pattern and a wallpaper.

2 Scroll through the Pattern list and choose the Circuits pattern.

The sample screen shows what this pattern will look like on your desktop.

3 Make sure that (None) appears in the Wallpaper list box.

If you have a wallpaper selected, it might cover up the pattern. Some of the wallpaper options do not take up the entire desktop, so they can have a pattern behind them.

4 Choose Apply.

Choosing Apply changes the background pattern so you can see what it will look like without closing the dialog box first (see Figure 6.6). Another way to customize the appearance of your desktop background is to add wallpaper to it or change the wallpaper currently displayed.

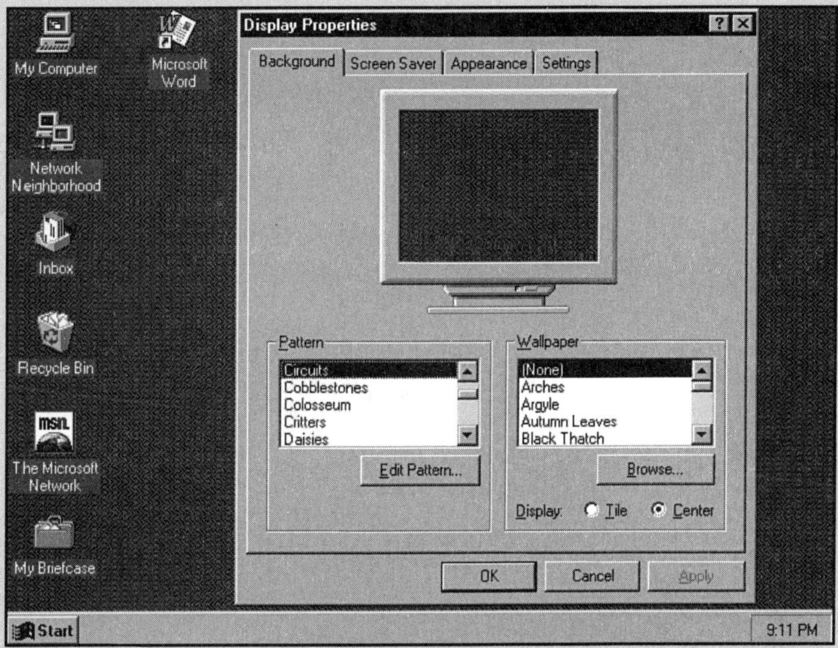

Figure 6.6
The Circuits pattern on the desktop.

5 In the Pattern list box, choose (None).

This gives you a "clean slate" to work with so you can see how the wallpaper alone will look on the desktop.

6 Choose Blue Rivets in the Wallpaper list box.

The sample screen shows a rough approximation of how this wall-paper will look on your desktop.

7 Click the Tile option button.

The Tile option will "tile" the pattern across the screen so it fills the screen completely.

8 Choose Apply.

Choosing Apply tiles the wallpaper across the desktop so you can see if you like the new wallpaper. Your desktop should look like the one shown in Figure 6.7. Leave the desktop in this state for the next lesson, in which you learn how to adjust your computer's date and time.

continues

To Customize the Desktop (continued)

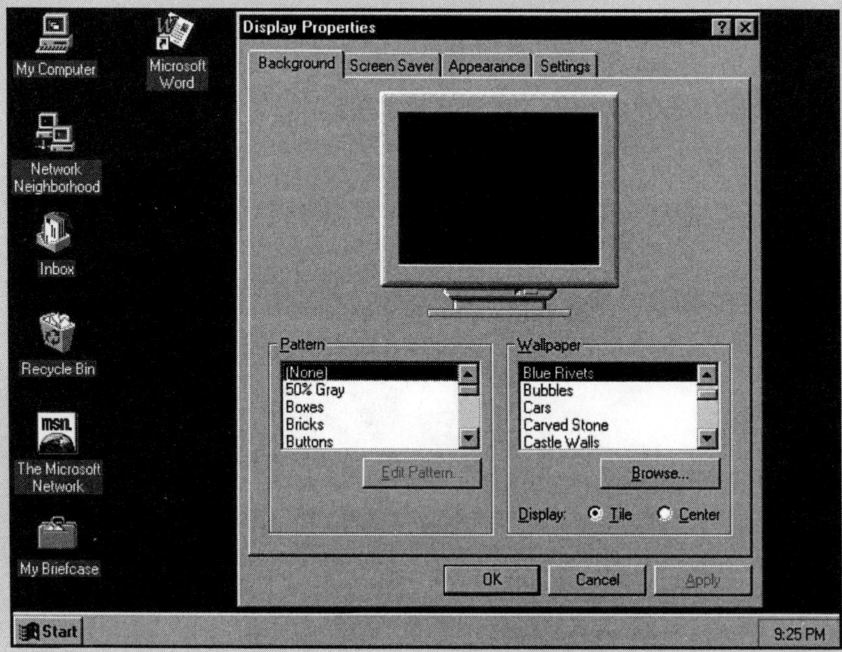

Figure 6.7
The Blue Rivets wallpaper on the desktop.

A large wallpaper looks best if you choose the **C**enter option button because the image appears in the middle of your desktop. If you have a small drawing, which looks better repeated throughout the desktop, choose the **T**ile button.

Wallpaper uses a great deal more memory than a solid color desktop or a pattern. If you have memory problems and use wallpaper, remove the wallpaper and choose a pattern. You can also choose the solid color desktop by choosing (None) for both the pattern and the wallpaper.

Lesson 3: Resetting the Date and Time

Your computer's internal clock keeps track of the date and time, which are then recorded with every file you save. In folder windows, you can see the date and time a file was saved. You can insert the current date and time into documents created with many applications. For example, you might insert the date in a header or footer of a document. The current time is displayed in the right corner of the taskbar. Obviously, it is important that the date and time are correct.

Usually, your computer maintains the date and time, but you should periodically check them to make sure they are still correct. If you change the battery in your computer, you might need to change the date or time. Change the date and time now.

To Reset Date and Time

1 Click the Start button and choose Settings.

The **S**ettings menu appears (see Figure 6.8).

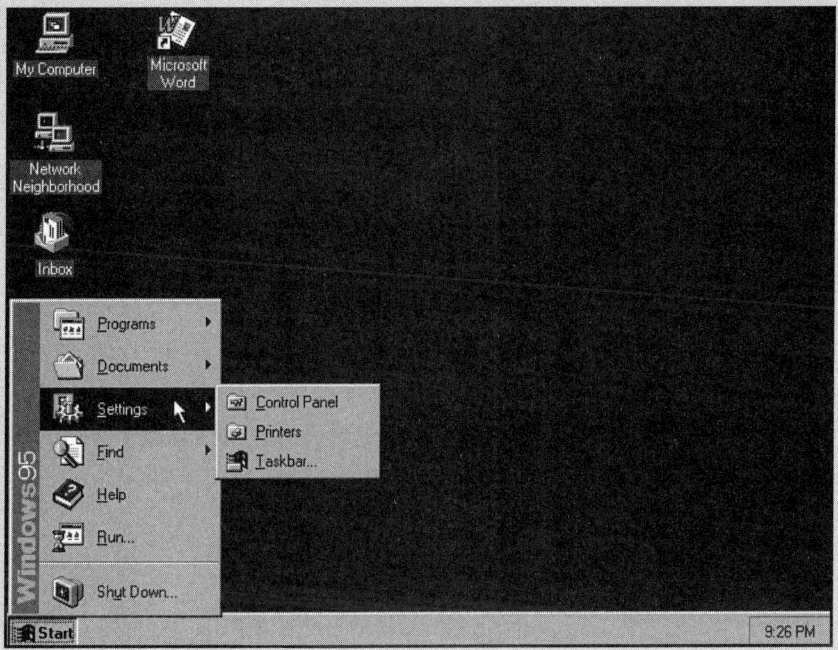

Figure 6.8
The **S**ettings menu.

2 Choose Control Panel.

Choosing **C**ontrol Panel opens the Control Panel window on the desktop (see Figure 6.9).

Figure 6.9
The Control Panel window.

continues

To Reset the Date and Time (continued)

3 Double-click the Date/Time icon.

The Date & Time page of the Date/Time Properties dialog box appears (see Figure 6.10). The left side of the dialog box shows you a calendar with the current date selected. The right side has both an analog and a digital indicator of the current time.

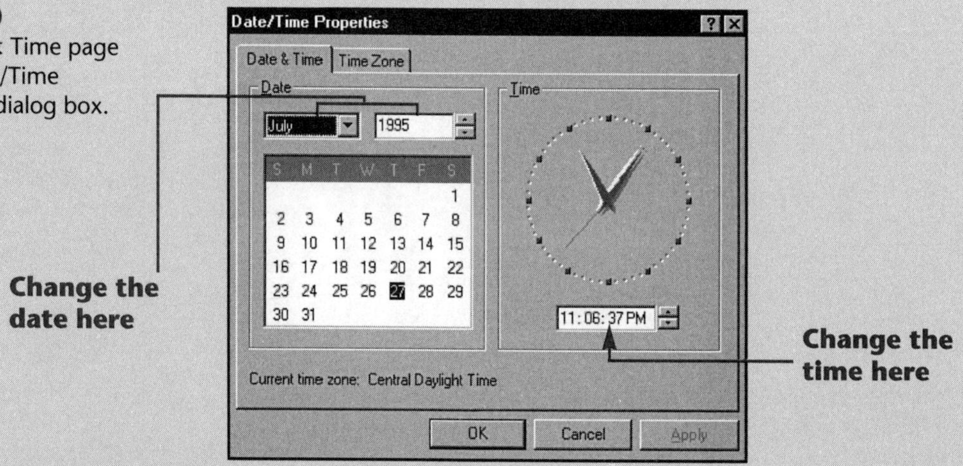

Figure 6.10 The Date & Time page in the Date/Time Properties dialog box.

4 Click the drop-down list arrow next to the current month; then choose February.

This changes the current month setting to February. The monthly calendar changes to show you the days of the month for February.

5 Click the up scroll arrow next to the current year to choose 1996.

This step isn't necessary if 1996 is already selected as the current year.

6 In the monthly calendar, click the number 1.

This changes the day to Thursday, the first of February. Now reset the system time.

7 Double-click the hour and type 1.

The current time is reset to 1 o'clock.

8 Double-click the minutes and type 50.

The current time is reset to 1:50. If you want, you can also set the seconds on the clock, but it isn't necessary. You can change the AM/PM setting if necessary by double-clicking AM or PM (whatever is currently displayed), then clicking the up or down scroll arrow. The dialog box should look like Figure 6.11.

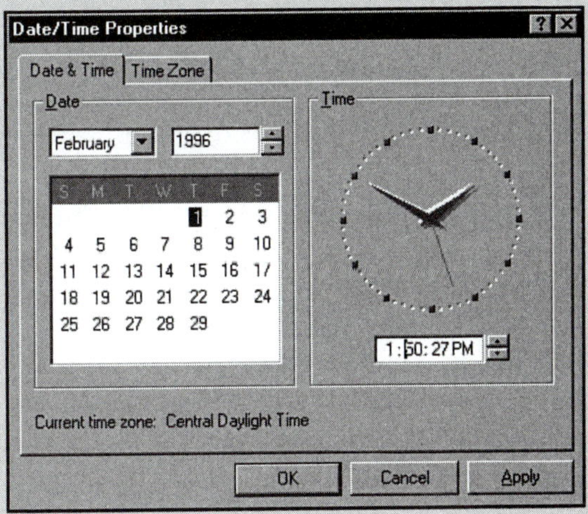

Figure 6.11
The Date & Time page with the new settings.

9 Change the date and time back to the correct settings.

This gives you a chance to practice the skills you learned in this lesson again as you reset the time.

10 Choose OK.

Choosing OK closes the Date/Time Properties dialog box and saves your changes. Leave the Control Panel window open for the next lesson, in which you learn how to change the mouse settings.

INSIDE Stuff

You can also double-click the current time on the taskbar to open the Date/Time Properties dialog box.

Lesson 4: Changing Mouse Settings

You can change mouse settings to make your mouse easier to work with. For example, you can modify the double-click speed so Windows recognizes your double-clicks. If your computer recognizes your double-clicks as two single clicks, you can change the speed of the clicks so it recognizes them as a double-click. If you are left-handed, you might want to change your primary mouse button to the right button to make it easier to use. Try changing the mouse settings now.

To Change Mouse Settings

1 In the Control Panel window, double-click the Mouse icon.

The Mouse Properties dialog box appears (see Figure 6.12).

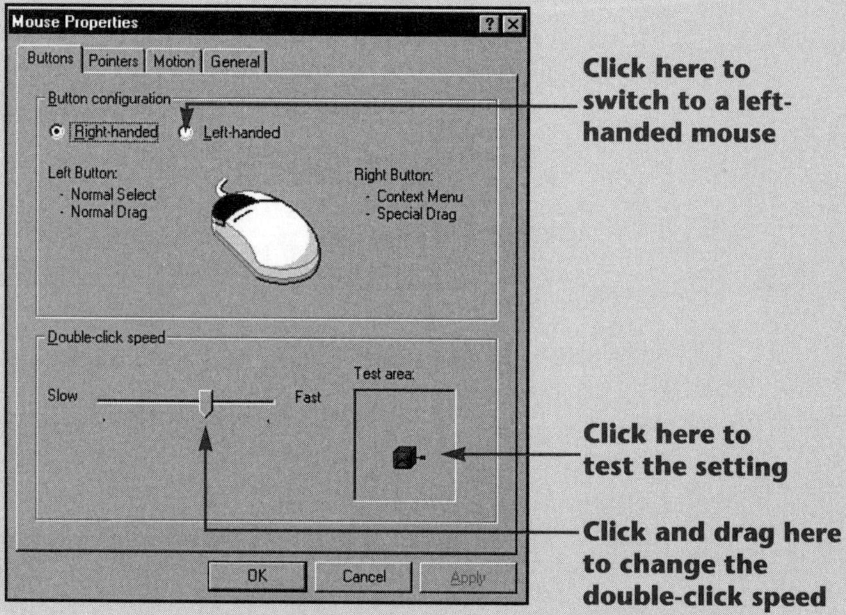

Figure 6.12
The Mouse Properties dialog box.

2 Click and drag the slider on the Double-click speed bar to the left.

This action slows down the double-click speed. In other words, you don't have to double-click as quickly to have Windows distinguish a double-click from two single clicks.

3 Double-click in the Test area box.

You can test the new speed in this box. If you double-click at the correct speed, the jack-in-the-box comes in and out of the box. Continue adjusting the double-click speed until you are satisfied with the response.

Another way to control the mouse settings is to switch the primary mouse button from the left button to the right button to make it easier for you to use your mouse. If you are left-handed, you might find the mouse more comfortable to use if you switch the primary mouse button. Switch the primary mouse button now.

4 Click the Left-handed option button.

Clicking this option button swaps the left and right mouse buttons so left-handed people can use the right button as the primary button. Notice that the sample mouse shows that the buttons are swapped. For now, swap the buttons back to their original positions.

5. **Click the Right-handed option button.**

6. **Choose OK.**

   Choosing OK closes the Mouse Properties dialog box and saves these settings.

7. **Close the Control Panel window.**

   Leave the desktop in this state for the next lesson, in which you learn how to add program and shortcut icons to the Startup folder.

Lesson 5: Add Shortcuts to the Startup Folder

The Startup folder, which is created during the installation of Windows 95, is used to store icons for items you want started each time you start Windows. These items can include programs and shortcuts to printers, folders, drives, and so on. If you want the My Computer window and the Printers folder open on the desktop each time you start Windows, add shortcuts to them in the Startup folder.

Another example: if you often use a calculator in your work, you can add this program icon to the Startup folder. When you start the Windows program, this programs starts too, so it's open on the desktop, ready for you to use. In this lesson, you add two program icons and one shortcut to the Startup folder.

To Add Shortcuts to the Startup Folder

1. **Open My Computer and double-click the drive C: icon.**

   Double-clicking a drive icon opens a window with the folders and files found on that drive. (If you need to review the steps to open My Computer, turn back to Lesson 1 in Project 3.)

2. **Scroll through the window and double-click the Windows folder icon.**

   Double-clicking the Windows folder icon opens a folder window with the subfolders and files within the Windows folder.

3. **Scroll through the window and double-click the Start Menu folder icon.**

   This opens the Start Menu folder window which has the Programs folder.

4. **Double-click the Programs folder icon.**

   This opens the Programs folder window which contains subfolders for Applications, Accessories, Main, Network, and Startup along with the shortcut icons that appear on the Programs menu.

continues

To Add Shortcuts to the Startup Folder (continued)

5 Double-click the Startup folder icon.

This opens the Startup folder window. In Figure 6.13, the Startup folder window is empty. Yours might already have shortcut icons that were added during the installation of a program, or that someone else added.

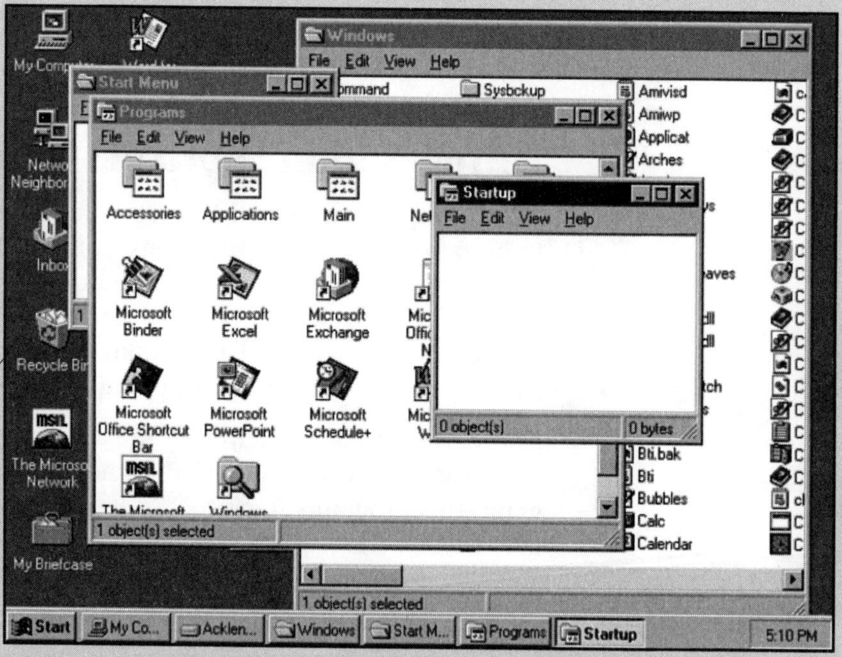

Figure 6.13
Add shortcuts to programs you want started automatically in the Startup folder.

6 Click the Windows folder window button on the taskbar.

This moves the Windows folder to the top of the stack.

7 Select the Calc and Pbrush files.

These are the two programs you want started automatically whenever you start Windows. (To select more than one file, click the first file, hold down Ctrl, then click the second file.)

8 Choose Edit, Copy.

This sends copies of the two files to the Windows Clipboard.

9 Click the Startup folder window button on the taskbar.

This moves the Startup folder window to the top of the stack where you can see it.

10 Choose Edit, Paste.

This copies the two program icons into the Startup folder.

11. **Click and drag the My Computer icon into the Startup folder window.**

Clicking and dragging the My Computer icon into the Startup folder window creates a shortcut for My Computer in the Startup folder.

A Shortcut message box appears, saying that you can't move or copy My Computer to that location and asks if you would like to create a shortcut to the item instead.

12. **Choose Yes.**

Choosing **Y**es creates the shortcut icon for My Computer and places it in the Startup folder. Your Startup folder window should look like the one shown in Figure 6.14. The next time you start Windows, the Calculator, Paint, and My Computer applications will start as well.

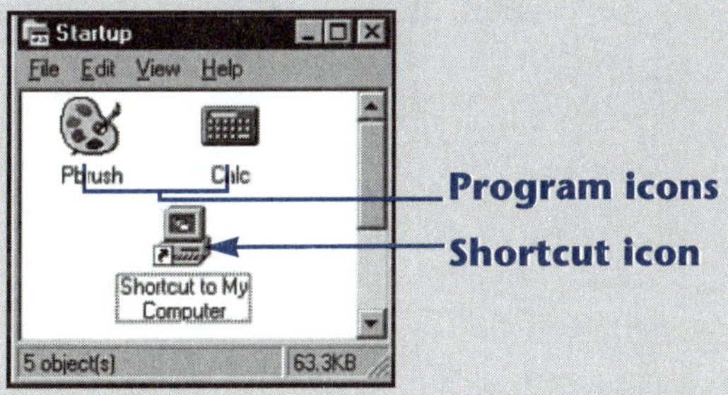

Figure 6.14 The Startup window with the Calculator, Paint, and My Computer icons in it.

13. **Close all the open windows.**

Leave the desktop in this state for the next lesson, in which you learn how to print files from Windows applications.

Lesson 6: Printing a File

For all Windows applications, the steps for printing a document are similar. Although the exact steps to follow might vary slightly, depending on which software package you are using, learning to print in one application makes it easy for you to print in another. In this lesson, you print a file from the WordPad application.

To Print a File

1 Use the Start button to open the Accessories menu, then choose the WordPad application.

2 Choose File, Print.

Print queue
A line of print jobs waiting to be printed.

The Print dialog box appears (see Figure 6.15). The name of the default printer—the printer to which Windows automatically prints—is displayed in the Print dialog box.

Choosing OK at this point sends the entire document to the *print queue*. This allows you to continue working while your file is being printed. Take a look at the other options available in the Print dialog box now.

Figure 6.15
The Print dialog box.

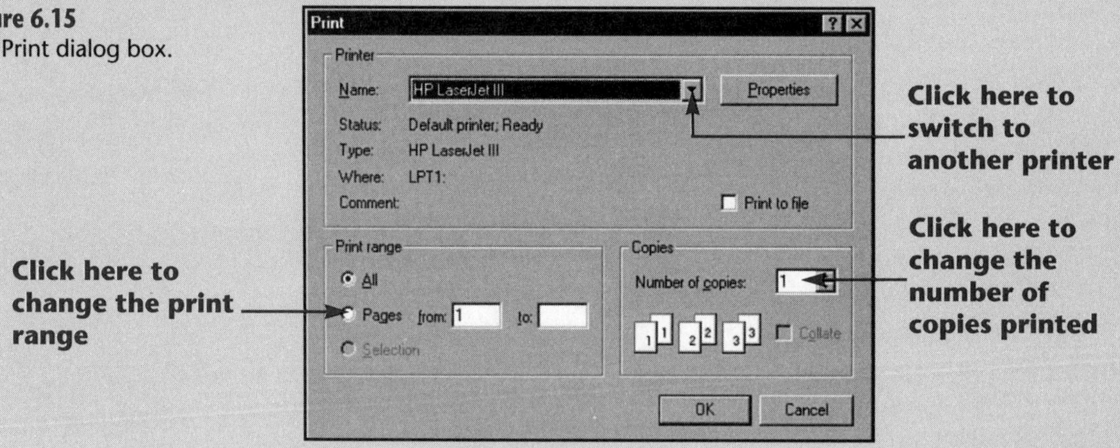

3 Click the Name drop-down list arrow.

A list of printers that have been installed in Windows appears. To switch to a different printer, click the printer name in the list.

4 Click the Name drop-down list arrow again.

Clicking the drop-down list arrow again closes the list of printers without selecting a different printer.

5 Click the Properties button.

The Properties dialog box for the default printer appears (see Figure 6.16).

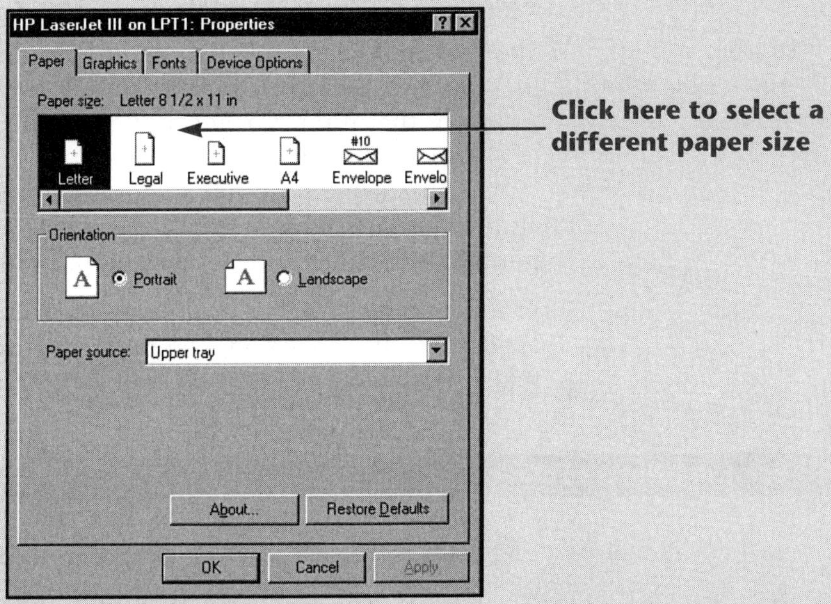

Figure 6.16
The Properties dialog box for the default printer.

6 Click the Legal icon in the Paper Size window.

The Legal page is now highlighted. Notice that several page sizes and several envelope sizes are available.

7 Click the Letter page in the Paper Size window.

You need to change the page size back to Letter; otherwise, your documents will print as if you had legal paper in your printer.

8 Choose OK.

Choosing OK returns you to the Print dialog box. As previously mentioned, choosing OK in the Print dialog box sends the entire document to the print queue.

9 Choose Cancel.

Choosing Cancel closes the Print dialog box without sending a document to the printer. This lesson is just for practice, so it isn't necessary to actually print the document.

Leave the WordPad application running for the next lesson, in which you learn how to cancel a print job from the Printers folder.

Lesson 7: Using the Printers Folder

Print job
A file that has been sent to the printer.

The Printers folder contains printer icons for each printer you have set up in Windows. Each printer icon opens a window that displays the print queue for that printer. You can use menu commands to pause the printing of a particular document or to pause printing to that printer. You can also cancel a particular print job if you sent it in error. Finally, you can clear out all the *print jobs* for a particular printer. You might use this option if your printer needs repair and you need to print to a different printer.

In the preceding lesson, you learned how to print a file from the WordPad application. In this lesson, you print a file from WordPad, open the Printers folder window for that printer, and cancel the print job.

To Use the Printers Folder

1. **Click the Start button, then choose Settings.**

   Clicking the My Computer icon opens the My Computer window.

2. **Choose Printers.**

   Choosing Printers opens the Printers folder window (see Figure 6.17). This folder window contains icons for each printer that has been installed in Windows.

Figure 6.17
The Printers folder.

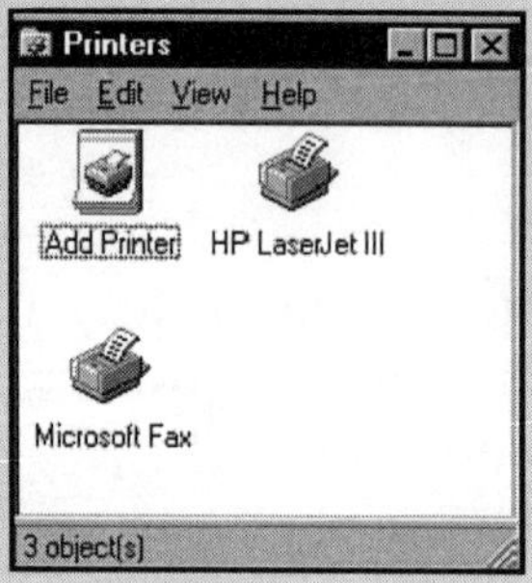

3. **Double-click the printer icon for your printer.**

   Double-clicking a printer icon opens a window that displays the print jobs for that printer. If you aren't sure which printer to choose, ask your instructor for assistance.

4. **Click the WordPad button on the taskbar.**

   Clicking the WordPad button moves the WordPad window to the top of the desktop. Open the LIGHT.DOC file in the sample file directory and print it now.

5. **Choose File, Open.**

   The **O**pen command opens the Open dialog box where you can look for the file you want to open (see Figure 6.18).

Figure 6.18
The Open dialog box.

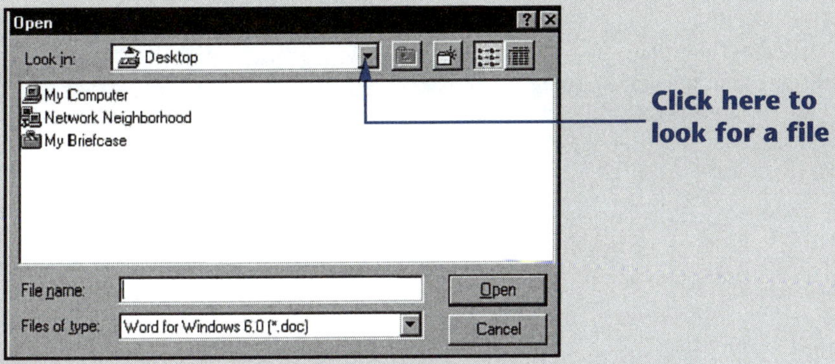

6 Click the Look In drop-down list arrow.

Clicking the drop-down list arrow opens a list of places where you can look for a file.

7 Click the hard drive icon.

Clicking the hard drive icon displays a list of folders on the hard drive (see Figure 6.19). By default, the Open dialog box in the WordPad application is set up to display Word for Windows 6.0 files with the extension .DOC.

Figure 6.19
The Open dialog box with a list of folders on the hard drive.

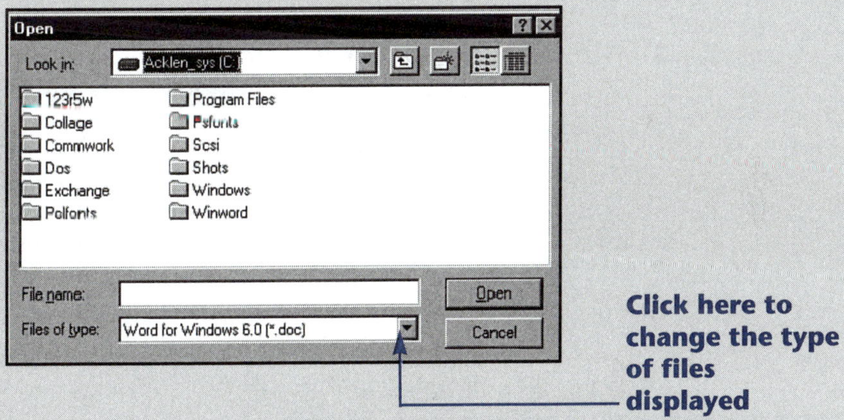

8 Double-click the LIGHT.DOC file.

Double-clicking a file name opens the file. You can also click the file to select it, and then click the Open button.

9 Choose File, Print, then press Enter.

This action send the entire document to the printer.

10 Click the taskbar button for the selected printer.

Clicking the taskbar button for the selected printer switches to the printer window where you can see the print job you just sent to the printer (see Figure 6.20).

continues

Figure 6.20
The LIGHT print job displayed in the window for the selected printer.

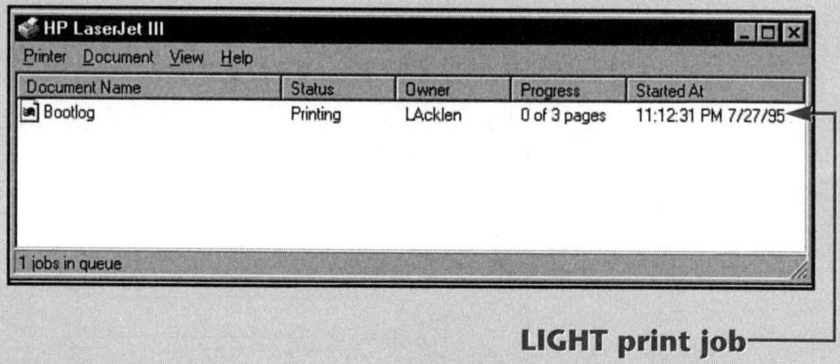

⑪ Click the LIGHT file.

Clicking the file selects it so you can take action on it. If you make a mistake when sending a file to print—for example, you print 100 copies instead of 10—you can delete the file from the print queue. Delete the file from the print queue now.

⑫ Press Del.

Even though you just deleted the print job, your printer might continue to print for a couple of minutes. The reason for this is that chunks of the print job are sent to the printer, where they are stored in the printer memory. Depending on the amount of printer memory installed in your printer, the memory might be able to store all or part of the print job. When the printer memory has been cleared, the print job stops printing.

If you have completed your session on the computer, shut down Windows before turning off the computer. When you shut down Windows, it automatically closes the open windows. Any unsaved files in the windows generate a message prompting you to save them. If you are prompted to save changes in the WordPad window, choose **N**o because you were just using the LIGHT file for practice. Otherwise, continue with the "Applying Your Skills" section.

Summary

To...	Do This
Change the screen saver	Right-click the desktop and choose P**r**operties.Click the Screen Saver tab. Click the **S**creen Saver drop-down list arrow, then choose a screen saver from the list. Specify a delay time in the **W**ait box. Choose OK.
Change the desktop pattern	Right-click the desktop and choose P**r**operties. Click the Background tab. Scroll through the **P**attern list box and choose a pattern. Make sure that (None) appears in the **W**allpaper list box. Choose OK.
Change the desktop wallpaper	Right-click the desktop and choose P**r**operties. Click the Background tab. Scroll through the **W**allpaper list box and choose a pattern. Make sure that (None) appears in the **P**attern list box. Click either the Tile or Center option button. Choose OK.
Reset the date and time	Click the Start button and choose **S**ettings. Choose **C**ontrol Panel. Double-click the Date/Time icon. To change the date: click the drop-down list arrow next to the current month and choose the correct month. Click the day of the month on the calendar to choose the correct day. To change the time, double-click the hour, then type the correct hour. Double-click the minutes, then type the correct minutes. It isn't necessary to specify the seconds (unless you want to). Choose OK.
Adjust the double-click speed of the mouse	Double-click the Mouse icon in Control Panel. Click and drag the slider on the **D**ouble-click speed bar. Move to the left to slow down the speed; move to the right to speed it up. Double-click in the Text area box. If you are double-clicking fast enough, jack-in-the-box pops in and out of the box. Choose OK.
Swap the mouse buttons	Double-click the Mouse icon in Control Panel. Click the **L**eft-handed option button. Choose OK.
Add an icon to the Startup folder	Open My Computer and double-click the drive C: icon. Double-click the Windows folder icon. Double-click the Start Menu folder icon. Double-click the Programs folder icon. Double-click the Startup folder icon. Click and drag icons into the Startup folder to add them to the folder.

To...	Do This
Print a file	Start the Windows program. Open the file you want to print. Choose **F**ile, **P**rint then choose OK.
Change to a different printer	From the Print dialog box, click the **N**ame drop-down list arrow. Select the printer in the list. Choose OK.
Change to a different paper size	From the Print dialog box, click the **P**roperties button. Click a page icon in the Paper Size window. Choose OK.
Open the Printers folder	Open My Computer and double-click the Printers icon; or open the Start menu and choose **S**ettings, then **P**rinters.
Delete a print job	In the Printers folder, double-click the printer icon that represents the printer you use. Right-click the print job in the list, choose Cancel Printing.
Pause a print job	In the Printers folder, double-click the printer icon that represents the printer you use. Right click the print job in the list, choose Pause Printing.

Applying Your Skills

These "On Your Own" exercises enable you to practice the skills you have learned in this project. Take a few minutes to work through these exercises now.

On Your Own

Customizing the Desktop

1. Change the screen saver in your computer by right-clicking the desktop to bring up the Context menu. Choose P**r**operties. Click the Screen Saver tab.
2. Change the screen saver to Flying Through Space.
3. Use the Se**t**tings button to increase the number and speed of the stars.
4. Change the **W**ait time to eight minutes. This is how long the keyboard or mouse must be idle before the screen saver comes on.
5. Preview the screen saver. Stop the preview by moving the mouse.
6. Click the Background tab to change the desktop's pattern and wallpaper. Select Bricks from the **P**attern list box.
7. Without exiting the dialog box, select Black Thatch from the **W**allpaper list box. Notice how the Bricks pattern is covered by the wallpaper.

8. Select (None) from the **W**allpaper list box so that the wallpaper is no longer layered over the pattern.
9. Click the Cancel button to close the dialog box without saving your changes to the settings.

Customizing the Mouse Settings

1. Open the Control Panel window by choosing **C**ontrol Panel from the **S**ettings menu.
2. Double-click the Mouse icon to open the Mouse Properties dialog box. Click the Motion tab.
3. Click the Sh**o**w Pointer Trails check box. Move the mouse pointer around in the dialog box to see the mouse trails. The mouse pointer can be hard to follow on some laptop screens. Mouse trails make it easier to find and follow the mouse pointer.
4. Click the Pointers tab and then click the **S**cheme drop-down list arrow. You can choose a pointer scheme from the list that appears. For example, if you prefer a larger pointer, you can choose Windows Standard (extra large) or (large).
5. Choose 3D Pointers. Notice the change in the pointers in the list box.
6. Choose Windows Standard (extra large) from the **S**cheme drop-down list. The larger pointers were designed to assist visually impaired users.
7. Click the Cancel button to close the Mouse Properties dialog box without saving your changes.

Changing the Date and Time Settings

1. Double-click the Date/Time icon in the Control Panel window. The Date/Time Properties dialog box appears.
2. Click the Time Zone tab and then click the drop-down list arrow.
3. Scroll up through the list and choose Alaska's time zone.
4. Change the time zone to Central Time.
5. Click the Date & Time tab. Change the date to your birthday. Click OK to make the change.
6. Double-click the current time button on the right side of the taskbar to open the Date/Time Properties dialog box again.
7. Change the time zone, date, and time back to their original settings.

Printing a Document

1. Open the WordPad application. (Hint: Choose Start, **P**rograms, Accessories, WordPad.)
2. Type the following sentence:

   Windows 95 is my FRIEND!
3. From the **F**ile menu, choose **P**rint.
4. Print two copies of the file.
5. Close the WordPad application.

INDEX

SYMBOLS

D

E–F

G–H

S

T

U–V

W–Z